MW00905099

Google VIDEO

"The Solution for Brain Injuries and Bankruptcies"

# THE EDUCATED CONSUMERS GUIDE TO
# NO-FAULT AUTOMOBILE INSURANCE

*How America can save billions in Medicaid costs
and create comprehensive and unlimited
medical benefits for life, for American's,
who are catastrophically injured
(brain and spinal cord injuries)
in automobile accidents!*

## IT'S YOUR FAULT IF YOU DON'T KNOW ABOUT NO-FAULT!

JOHN GWYNNE PROSSER II

authorHOUSE™

*1663 LIBERTY DRIVE, SUITE 200
BLOOMINGTON, INDIANA 47403
(800) 839-8640
WWW.AUTHORHOUSE.COM*

*First published by AuthorHouse 08/19/05*

*ISBN: 1-4208-8028-4 (e)*
*ISBN: 1-4208-5948-X (sc)*

*Library of Congress Control Number: 2005905371*

*Printed in the United States of America*
*Bloomington, Indiana*

*This book is printed on acid-free paper.*

**Why every Driver and Automobile passenger in America needs the Michigan model for "No-Fault" automobile insurance, and how it will save America *billions* of dollars in, Medicaid costs while providing comprehensive, compassionate, quality <u>in-home</u>**

**Nursing care and other services for the catastrophically injured.**

*Michigan is a great place to live, work, and raise a family.*

*We have massively superior automobile insurance which you can create in your state!*

*Or You could just move here!*

## *The New Paradigm:*

*Unlimited medical benefits* and *rehabilitation,* for automobile accident victims. The insurance will simultaneously reduce unnecessary, costly, and lengthy litigation. The insurance will let people live with dignity and save America *billions of dollars* in Medicaid costs. The Michigan model is a compassionate, spiritually mature and an economically viable solution to the crushing reality hundred's of thousands of drivers now experience.

*I am writing this book because I know the Michigan scheme is superior to any other scheme anywhere. I know that if people read about what if offers and covers that they will want it for themselves and their loved ones. Everyone in America needs this insurance. It is so important that it should be studied by every American driver and understood immediately in order to gain the <u>absolutely necessary benefits</u> offered by the coverage. Then individuals in every state can <u>educate their legislators and Governors</u>, compelling them to* *provide the leadership for this initiative and adopt this scheme in their state.*

*My purpose in writing this book is to educate and stimulate discussion among all American citizens, President Bush, our State Governors, and Healthcare providers, our State legislators and accident victims. My ultimate purpose is to stimulate positive legislative action by every driver in America and every leader in America to bring about the significant and favorable change in every states statute that will manifest the powerful change I recommend.*

## Introduction:

Presently the only state in America which provides *lifetime unlimited medical benefits* for individuals catastrophically injured in an automobile accident is MICHIGAN. This automobile insurance benefit is called Personal Injury Protection (PIP) in Michigan. Recently a national study hailed Michigan's no-fault system, the Insurance Research Council (www.Ircweb.org) observed that **insurance rates and claim losses are lower in Michigan** than in other no-fault auto insurance states between the years of 1997 to 2002. In 2002 the average auto insurance expenditure in Michigan was just $839.00 compared to New York $1,087.00, Colorado $914.00, and Florida $870.00. This proves that Michigan has the best no-fault insurance system in the nation!

Michigan is the only state in the nation to offer unlimited medical and rehabilitation services, yet maintains insurance rates close to the national average. During the same time period the study found that the average amounts that personal injury protection claimants reported for expenses stemming from their injuries increased 122% in Colorado, 60% in New York, 37% in Florida, and just 2% in Michigan. The study also found average costs for certain medical treatments is some no-fault states sometimes more than double the cost for similar treatment in other no-fault states. You can find information regarding insurance costs and issues at the website for the **Insurance Information Institute at:** (www.iii.org).

One of the goals of no fault auto insurance systems is to alleviate pressure on court systems by reducing tort liability claims for minor injuries. Presently if you do not have this Michigan coverage, meaning <u>you live in a state other than Michigan</u>, and you or a loved one is catastrophically injured; you will exhaust your health insurance coverage then begin to spend your assets until they are exhausted (bankruptcy, or just short of it) at which point you can apply for Medicaid. **Medical bills cause an average of two million bankruptcies a year according to a study by Harvard Medical School**. Of the bankruptcy's in 2001 used for the study, most of those who filed had health insurance. You can go to google.com and put in "Harvard study medical bankruptcy" or go to this link <u>http://content. healthaffairs.org/cgi/content/full/hlthaff.w5.63/DC1</u>

Once you qualify for Medicaid you will then realize the benefit available is wholly inadequate to satisfy the needs of the injured party. The shortage of nurses as a profession complicates the issue further, for they desire to optimize their income and find pay rates offered by the Medicaid system significantly lower than every other sector in healthcare resulting in <u>a super acute shortage of nurse staff for Medicaid</u> recipients. Presently **Medicaid costs are soaring** across America and are presenting a significant financial burden to most State and Federal governments. On the subject of Nurses it seems to me that our society has forgotten what a blessed profession Nursing is! I believe we should say thank you more often to the profession that provides 90% of the TLC and all of the bedside care that patients receive. I believe you will really appreciate them if and when you actually need them.

Currently in Michigan if you are in an automobile accident and Medicaid eligible, your medical expenses are paid for by the auto insurer, not Medicaid. What will happen to Medicaid costs and the quality of life for catastrophically injured patients if every state in America adopts a scheme for automobile insurance based on the Michigan model? I predict it will save America **billions of dollars** in Medicaid costs and provide a massively superior quality of life for those injured and their families as well. Quality and comprehensive health care is achievable for all accident victims for life if the Michigan model is enacted in every state. In Michigan you receive unlimited medical benefits *and rehabilitation for LIFE.* Presently in America there is a **silent epidemic**, <u>every year</u> there are in excess of 1.5 million people who sustain traumatic brain injuries, <u>44% of</u> <u>those occur from vehicle accidents</u>, among the survivors 80,000 cope with life-long losses of function. Additionally, 2000 people will exist in a persistent vegetative state.

**STARTLING TRUTH,** brain injuries kill more Americans under the age of 34 than all others combined! The Michigan Brain Injury Association (<u>www.biami.org</u>) holds the largest annual conference in America for any state association. In 2004, more than 1000 individuals registered for the two day event. The Michigan Brain Injury Association (<u>www. BIAUSA.org</u>) provides help, hope, and a voice for the 200,000 Michigan residents who live with a permanent disability as a result of a brain injury. To get a free copy of a valuable resource on traumatic brain injury (TBI) called **'TBI Survival Guide'** please visit www. tbiguide.com. You can also find an executive summary of the Michigan department of community health, traumatic brain injury project report, September 2004, at www.michigan.gov , go to long term care then search for "tbi". This report outlines the extensive needs and lack of resource for people who have brain injuries that are not related to automobile accidents and their accompanying insurance coverage.

**Cost drivers in insurance:** Besides increasing medical costs each year, there are more than two million car accidents involving injuries. Typical costs for treating an automobile accident victim ranges from $6,000.00 to $9,000.00 but can easily run into the tens of thousands of dollars. Millions of dollars if the victim is catastrophically injured.

Higher jury awards in vehicular liability cases are putting upward pressure on automobile insurance rates. The average jury award in automobile liability cases did increase from $187,000.00 in 1994 to $323,000.00 in 2001, an increase of 73% according to the most recent data from jury verdict research. In fact, automobile liability issues are much more important than most people realize, about 60% of USA automobile premiums paid in 2003 (more than $80 billion) were for liability coverage. The average cost for automobile insurance nationwide for 2004 is estimated at $871.00 per year. Automobile insurers nationwide will only pay between 15 and 20 billion dollars in medical claims.

**Medicaid threatens to overwhelm every state in America:** This challenge is more than a looming crisis created by real economic needs, it is also a huge dilemma which is fed by the reduced revenues due to lower tax collections on slow economic growth. According to the National Governors Association, states expect to spent 12% more on average this year, 2005, than they did last year. It is reported that 70% of the Medicaid budget is spent on the blind, the elderly and the disabled. While the balance, 30%, covers poor families with children and moms to be. I believe an analysis of the Medicaid costs associated with care for those individuals who are **catastrophically injured in auto accidents will be in the billions.** You can find information on Medicaid issues at the Kaiser Family Foundation website www.KFF.org

**WHAT IF ONE OF THE ACCIDENT VICTIMS HAPPEN TO BE YOU OR ONE OF YOUR LOVED ONES?**

**WHAT IS THE MEDICAL COVERAGE PROVIDED BY YOUR AUTOMOBILE INSURANCE?**

**WOULD YOU HAVE ENOUGH FINANCIAL RESOURCE TO MEET THE NEED?**

**<u>MOSTLIKELY, YOU DO NOT!</u>  You would do well to start talking to your state legislators.**

# Contact your:

Governor, State Representative, and State Senator and *send them a copy of this book.*

Make it happen and become a force for powerful good, work enthusiastically to educate  your legislature, and find a sponsor for a bill to change the automobile insurance law in  your state.  If you network with your family and friends via email, you can direct people  to specific websites and they once again network  with their family and friends, and so on, everyone can contribute to the solution of an enormous problem. It is crucial to  contact local state Senators and State Representatives. Please get educated on this issue  now and help make powerful and positive changes—you just might need them!

 America needs leadership on this issue! You can and should become a catalyst for this positive change!

# Michigan's No-Fault Automobile Insurance Scheme

## The No-Fault Automobile Insurance Act (MCL 500.3101), adopted by the Michigan

Legislature in 1972, is unique not only in the benefits provided for, but also in its own club of around a dozen states who have no-fault insurance. A copy of the public act from the Michigan compiled laws database is available at the back of the book, or visit the website www.cis.state.mi.us/ins . More information can be found at www.legislature.mi.gov or www. michiganlegislature.org, when there go directly to laws, then click frequent requests, then insurance, and then auto no fault, where you will find a complete outline and complete chapters of the law.

The simplicity of the no-fault idea is that it provides benefits to anyone injured in an automobile accident regardless of who is at fault. It also limits your ability to recover damages against the party at fault if you are the victim of the accident. In Michigan, you give up the right to sue in an automobile accident except when someone is killed or seriously injured. Because of this, payment for medical bills will not be held up by the massively slow grind of the courts. You should most definitely buy high limits on your liability portion of your insurance which pays others damages if you happen to be at fault **and** allows you to collect excess wage loss and compensation for pain and suffering through your own insurance if another at fault driver strikes you and they have low limits of coverage. A good level would be a minimum of $100,000.00 per person and $300,000.00 per accident. Optimum would be $300,000.00 and $500,000 respectively.

In Michigan the benefits you are entitled to, personal injury protection (PIP) benefits, are also known as personal protection insurance benefits. Of significant note is that in its singular wisdom the Michigan legislature drafted a statute that is a "fee for services plan", not a managed/rationed care plan.

# There are four main categories of benefits under the Michigan model.

The most significant in my opinion is "allowable medical expenses", which **provides** <u>Unlimited medical expenses</u> and rehabilitation benefits for life. These expenses are for all reasonable charges that are incurred for **"reasonably necessary"** products, services and accommodations for an injured person's care, recovery or rehabilitation. According to the office of the Michigan insurance commissioner, "The Michigan no-fault system was adopted in 1973 to increase the level of benefits paid to injured persons, make sure such payments are made promptly, and reduce the proportion of premium dollars paid out for legal and administrative costs". I believe the Michigan legislature created a superior **model for insurance benefits**. And, in doing so, assure a <u>dignified quality</u>

<u>of life</u> for <u>catastrophically injured patients</u> and one that does not create a financial hardship regarding medical bills for the families of those patients. It is argued by many that there is still need for clearer language in the statute pertaining to certain issues, and I agree.

However, without question, Michigan's law is the absolute best insurance policy you can own in America if you should need it, and God forbid, you or a family member just might need it. Please review your current coverage and determine if it is adequate.

# The BIG FOUR MAJOR Benefits:

**1. Allowable medical expenses.** Under section 3107, an injured person covered by this insurance is entitled to allowable expenses which are defined as "all reasonable charges incurred for <u>reasonably necessary</u> products, services and accommodations for an injured person's care, recovery or rehabilitation". These benefits are unlimited in duration and cost. Some of the benefits or services you can expect include medical expenses such as hospital expenses, prescriptions, doctor fees, medical equipment, therapies (including psychological, rehabilitation, speech and occupational services, in home attendant or nursing care). Other benefits include, but may not be limited to, all reasonable generated hospital fees, medical equipment, prescriptions, doctor charges, prosthetic devices, psychological service, chiropractic care, and any other reasonably necessary medical expenses.

**A) Home Modifications:** If your residence should need renovations in order to accommodate the injured party's physical condition, this is also covered. It is often necessary to create modifications in the residence to accommodate a catastrophically injured person's new needs. Sometimes this involves a new suite built as an addition, expansion of room/hallway/ or door, and/or an entirely new residence with appropriate modifications to be built. There are multiple factors which decide whether you actually hold title to the residence, room and board expenses, and compensation for maintenance in the home.

**B) In-home Nursing Care including Attendant Care:** These services can include registered nurses and licensed practical nurses who are skilled care and/or high-tech home health aides or CENA's (competency evaluated nurse's aide) who are considered unskilled, and/or home health aides, or a combination of both. The services provided can include bathing, feeding, all aides to daily living, transportation to physicians and **rehabilitation** services, as well as in home therapies including **physical therapy, speech therapy, occupational therapy**, and any reasonable and customary needs the injured person may have.

The nursing care may be provided 24 hours per day as long as the need persists.

The services provided by a home health care company can include feeding, turning, wound care, range of motion exercises, toileting, catheter

4

insertion, skincare and many other services. Many accident victims are on ventilators and paralyzed, fed by G-tubes, or given medications by J-tubes, brain injured and spinal cord injured. Some require care by multiple staff 24 hours per day 7 days per week on a year round basis. Others who are brain injured, yet ambulatory, require constant companionship to assist them with their need for direction through prompting as well as to manage behavioral deficits associated with the brain injury.

## **HOMECARE**

While it is possible for your loved one to go to a facility for long term care, many doctors, psychologists and families believe that the home environment is the best

environment to nurture an accident victim spiritually, mentally, emotionally and socially. I believe that, if asked, most people would choose for themselves or their loved ones to be in their home.

**C) Rehabilitation:** The medical benefits includes physical rehabilitation, as well as the expense of vocational rehabilitation, job training and job placement. **In Michigan, there are many outstanding rehabilitation services and facilities,** largely due to the Michigan automobile no-fault law and the financial resources it provides our citizens. **Michigan has acute care centers, sub-acute care**

**centers,** respite care centers, and long-term care centers designed specifically to serve the complex needs of the catastrophically injured. Michigan health care providers offer the very best care for brain injuries and spinal cord injuries, and they have an accumulative experience **serving patients that is unparalleled anywhere in America.**

**D) Transportation:** It is also a benefit, if it is reasonably necessary for an injured person's care, recovery or rehabilitation, to purchase a modified van to serve the needs of the patient. Many spinal cord injured patients confined to a gurney or wheelchair require special transportation to get around.

**2. Work Loss Benefits:** In Michigan when your are unable to work due to an automobile accident, wage loss benefits are payable for up to 3 years. The allowable amounts are 85% of gross pay, including overtime. Up to a maximum of $4,293.00 per month, as of September 2004.

**3. Replacement Service Expenses:** In Michigan you are also entitled to receive reimbursement for expenses as the result of having to pay others to perform services that the injured party would have ordinarily performed, up to $20.00 per day for a duration of 3 years. Some of those items covered would include house maintenance, yard work, laundry, and general housekeeping.

**4. Survivor's Loss Benefits:** If an automobile accident causes death, the dependents of the decedent are entitled to receive survivor's loss benefits which include funeral and burial expenses. The benefit also includes wage loss for 3 years up to the maximum allowed, $4,000.00, as well as replacement services at $20.00 per day. The one caveat is you must be a dependent of the decedent.

In addition to these benefits, a very significant service that the catastrophically injured receive in Michigan is ***Case Management***. Case Management is a service where a 'case manager' most often a Registered Nurse provides an injured individual and their family with experienced and professional leadership as a patient advocate for all of their concerns and needs. You can think of a case manager as your Healthcare Coordination Consultant.

Typically a case manager will be requested by the Attorney or by the insurance company adjuster to visit with the family while they are in the hospital in order to understand all of the clinical issues involved in the patient's care and understand all of the pre-morbid circumstances of the patient's life including psycho-social dynamics and idiosyncratic issues.

Subsequent to a gaining of a thorough understanding, it is typical that the case manager will identify the resources to satisfy the patient's needs. This may include sub-acute rehabilitation facilities, homecare nursing services, durable medical equipment, prescriptions, home modifications, wheelchair accessible vans, and physical, speech and occupational therapies. There is also the identification of specialized physicians like physiatrists who are doctors that specialize in physical medicine and rehabilitation. Case managers, in my experience, can be very much like a guardian angel for patients and their families, the primary function of case management is patient advocacy. I know that in Michigan we have hundred's of excellent case managers, many of whom are experienced registered nurses, and this resource is available because of our superior insurance scheme which provides the financial resources to pay for these quality of life services.

## How is all of this Unlimited Benefits accomplished?

## The funding comes directly from the consumers of the insurance!

<u>The Michigan Catastrophic Claim Association</u> (reinsurance), created under section 3104 of the Michigan No-Fault Act. (a copy of the plan of operation can be accessed at <u>www.michigan.gov</u> then go to "the office of financial and insurance services" tab, then in search box type : Michigan Catastrophic claims association plan of operation, then select go, then select result #4, then select #2, it will be interesting to read them all.

The automobile insurance companies in Michigan allocate a portion of the premiums paid by all drivers to reinsure themselves and those of us who are insured, through the MCCA thus capping their payout on any claim at $350,000.00 (2004) which virtually guarantees them excellent profitability and allows them to easily manage their reserves. It is a win/win system!

Once an injured person passes that cap on costs, every nickel spent on care is reimbursed to the insurer by the Michigan Catastrophic Claim Association. The MCCA collects approximately $140.00 annually per automobile presently. Multiply that number by approximately 7.2 million automobiles means taking in approximately $1,008,000,000.00. They reportedly spend $636,000,000.00 annually, according to the calculations, resulting in excess for the fund, which with compounding interest, compounding over the years has produced significant excess resource dollars! Historically our legislature in Michigan even refunded several billion dollars of that excess, I believe that the *refund is a mistake.* I believe if every policy holder were aware of this mechanism to assure abundant resource in the event they or a loved one required it, they would surely vote to keep the excess in the fund! Presently it is reported that there is $45 billion dollars in catch loss reserves, which is equal to being the 54$^{th}$ largest for GNP of the 208 reporting countries of the world. This money is the policy holder's money and it is wise investment on their part even if it is required by statute. It is intended to provide the security of unlimited medical benefits and rehabilitation for life so that you or your loved one can live with <u>dignity</u> and <u>ample resources</u> for care and improvement. <u>This coverage also eliminates the</u> <u>terrible economic burdens lain upon families who do not have it</u>. A buyer's guide to automobile insurance can be accessed at <u>www.cis. state.mi.us/ins</u>. The Michigan office of the Insurance Commissioner. The MCCA has 8 billion in assets. The MCCA has paid 4 billion in claims since inception through December 2004. Brain injury accounts for 53% of all claims.

**Underinsured motorist coverage:** This benefit allows you to buy additional coverage on your policy so that if you are injured by another driver who is notably at fault, and they have very small limits on their coverage, you can pursue additional economic damages through your policy. **(A must have coverage.)**

**Uninsured motorist coverage:** This benefit allows you to buy additional coverage on your policy so that in the event you are hit and injured by a driver of a vehicle which has no insurance coverage you can seek additional compensation for your non-economic damages. This is referred to as a liability claim. The law is very clear in Michigan, if you are the owner or registrant of a vehicle which is involved in an accident and you are uninsured, you cannot collect no-fault PIP benefits. If you buy this coverage, this will compensate you for pain and suffering and excess wage loss. This coverage applies only if a hit and run vehicle or an uninsured motorist strikes you. **(A must have coverage.)**

**Uncoordinated medical benefits** and **Full wage loss:** In Michigan you can purchase either a **full benefits** or coordinated benefits no-fault insurance policy. When you purchase a full benefits policy, the insurance company is contractually required to pay your no-fault benefits, even though those benefits may be payable under another health insurance policy you may have, effectively making no-fault insurance the primary provider of health care benefits for your medical needs as a result of your accident. Now keep in mind the premium for full coverage costs a little more and it is certainly worth it if you need it. Many families have told me it was a nightmare emotionally, spiritually, and mentally at their time of need, to have a coordinated policy because of the labyrinthine paperwork and phone call process associated with it. I highly recommend **uncoordinated coverage, full wage and full medical.**

I believe there are too many Michiganders who have coordinated policies simply because they do not fully understand the implications and are attracted to saving a few dollars, (in my opinion an uninformed decision at best). If you do have a coordinated medical benefit and have Blue Cross Blue Shield, an HMO, or a PPO, your health care providers will have to first bill that insurer for the maximum benefit allowed and use providers in the network, then the automobile no-fault insurance will cover the excess costs. **When you buy uncoordinated you can pursue services from any provider**. When it is coordinated, you must first pursue the in-network providers assigned by your health insurer and exhaust your benefit with them, then you can pursue any provider under your no-fault insurance. If you do have a health insurer with language in your contract that makes it secondary to no-fault insurance, that obviously conflicts with what you purchased from your automobile insurer. In that instance, the Michigan Supreme Court has ruled that where a conflict exists, the health insurer is primary and the automobile insurer is secondary. When your health insurance is coordinated and your automobile insurance is uncoordinated, then your automobile insurance is primary. Now if you have un-coordinated policies in both instances, health and automobile, it is legally permitted to collect from both for medical costs.

**Points of interest regarding homecare under Michigan no-fault:**  A typical story of a person catastrophically injured in an automobile accident. We begin the story at the scene of the accident where typically automobile a. ran into automobile b. The collision results in significant physical damage to the vehicles and the individuals. Emergency medical services and the police arrive, the extent of the injuries is ascertained, the injured people are transferred to the closest level one trauma center (also known as an acute care facility/hospital). Often enough the injured are taken to emergency and there they are stabilized. A battery of tests ensues and vital signs are closely monitored. The family is contacted. Soon thereafter, the family arrives and gets insight as to the extent of the injury. Often there is emergency surgery, long stays in the intensive care unit and even unconsciousness for the accident victim. This process is emotionally overwhelming and is accompanied by feelings of anger, fear, sadness, and dread of the unknown. These intense emotions often visit the family of the injured not to mention the injured. This terrible scenario is often compounded if the person is a parent and/or the breadwinner for the family. Typically 99 of the 100 people do not know what their automobile insurance coverage provides, nor do they know what the limits of coverage are or how all of this is going to impact the family. Once a determination of the medical status of the injured person has been made, plans are made to transfer them to a sub-acute facility or rehabilitation facility for constant medical attention and therapies. All of this process is overwhelming, psychologically, emotionally, spiritually and physically.

The hospital wants to know the minute the family walks in the door, how this service will be paid for, will ask you to sign and personally guarantee the payment for services even when you present your health insurance and automobile insurance information.

Remember, if you do not live in Michigan, your automobile insurance medical coverage is already wholly inadequate and your medical coverage through your health insurance has its limits. This leads you to spend your own cash until you can qualify for Medicaid, which is based on financial need, meaning you are without anymore assets other than your home, car, and about $2,000.00 cash. You will spend your own cash for all of the costs I have already outlined, which are covered by Michigan's no-fault insurance scheme.

Now, once you plan to leave the sub-acute or rehabilitation facility and go home, will your insurances pay for attendant care services needed 24 hours per day 7 days a week? That can cost $15,000.00 to $35,000.00 per month depending on the skill level of staff required to care for your loved one. **Another one of the benefits under the Michigan scheme is that loved ones of the injured person can provide some of the attendant care services in the home and be compensated for that care.**

I have spent the past 12 years as the Vice-President of Health Partners. We provide nursing services in the home specializing in brain and spinal cord injuries. We help families find their way through their challenges and help them develop a plan for their daily needs and assist families with this type of in-home health care provided by our aide and nursing staff that actually care for these patients in their homes. We have seen every challenge and every obstacle and have creatively endeavored to enhance the quality of life for these injured people. I can tell you that the experience of suffering a catastrophic injury and/or having a loved one experience one is the most challenging experience that anyone could have. I believe this solution "The Michigan Model" will satisfy the needs of hundreds of thousands of Americans if not millions in the next 20 years.

Typically catastrophically injured patients will receive in-home therapies including range of motion therapies, skin care, physical therapy, speech therapy, and occupational therapy which includes learning adaptive skills for navigating the home with the new limitations. Sometimes patients have psychological and social circumstances which prohibit their return to their home so they need a residence where they can live and rehabilitate. Michigan has many of these. Because we have the most excellent insurance scheme in Michigan, we have abundant resources which have evolved from a desire to serve the needs of people who have terrible injuries from accidents including **physiatrists**, doctors who specialize in physical medicine and rehabilitation with specialized knowledge in brain and spinal cord injuries, neurologists and neuropsychologists, who through their vast experience understand the special needs of and provide treatment for patients with brain and spinal cord injuries.

Michigan's rehabilitation facilities are equipped with state of the art therapies and compassionate experienced therapists. There is also an abundance of long-term care residential facilities that specialize in the care required for the catastrophically injured and abundant in-home nursing care with the expertise and experience needed to serve patients with complex care needs. These services can and do address the enormously stressful circumstances which accompany significant injuries.

I am also one of the owners of a residence for the brain and spinal cord injured called **The Grand Home of Marshall** which offers individuals an outstanding environment to receive very specialized care. This is a resource born of our compassionate awareness of the need injured patients present and a sincere desire to serve those needs. We offer a team of professionals with decades of experience. We offer a team of professionals with decades of experience. We offer focused daily care and an enthusiasm for quality service. We have been encouraged by insurance companies and case managers and families to provide this very special program for individuals who often do not have a residence of their own and/or who are better served in an environment designed just for them. If you are interested in our residence or our homecare services, I can be reached via e-mail at JPROSSER123@comcast.net. I will be happy to answer any questions and send you a power point presentation. Our residence is a beautifully remodeled Queen Ann Victorian home located in the Historic heart of the city. We provide community re-entry programs, rehabilitation services, and structured living for short or long term residents. We offer personalized services in a Home environment.

A new study by the National Institute of Nursing research, one of the National Institutes of Health, appeared in the May 2004 issue, of the journal of American geriatrics society.

The Study shows that the elderly who receive specialized care throughout their hospital stay and at home following hospital discharge, those patients have a better quality of life and have fewer hospital readmissions! Instead of costing more money for this **specialized care**, the study showed that the care resulted in a nearly 38% savings in medicare costs!

# MICHIGAN CATASTROPHIC CLAIMS ASSOCIATION
## PLAN OF OPERATION

## ARTICLE I
### Name

**1.01.** The name of this unincorporated, non-profit association of insurers shall be the Michigan Catastrophic Claims Association (hereinafter referred to as the "Association").

## ARTICLE II
### Purpose

**2.01.** It is the purpose of the Association to implement Act No. 136, Public Acts of 1978, being Section 3104 of the Michigan Insurance Code of 1956, as amended, MCLA 500.3104, creating a Catastrophic Claims Association to indemnify members against ultimate loss in excess of the applicable amount set forth in Section 3104(2) of the Michigan Insurance Code, sustained under the statutorily required personal protection insurance coverages under policies of insurance providing the security required by section 3101(1) of the Michigan Insurance Code for the owners and registrants of motor vehicles required to be registered in the State of Michigan, resulting from each loss attributable to an accident which occurs on or after July 1, 1978.

**2.02.** Nothing in this Article II shall be construed to enlarge or otherwise affect the rights and obligations of the association or its Members and 3103 Members as specified in the following sections of this Plan or in the Michigan Insurance Code of 1956, as amended.

## ARTICLE III
### Effective Date

**3.01.** This Plan of Operation shall become effective on the date on which both of the following conditions shall have been satisfied: (i) The Commissioner issues written approval of this Plan or, if not sooner disapproved by written order of the Commissioner, thirty days has elapsed after the date of its submission to the Commissioner, and (ii) this Plan has been approved by majority vote of the Board and ratified by majority vote of the members, each member being allotted the number of votes equal to the number of its total Earned Car Years during the preceding calendar year.

## ARTICLE IV
### Definitions

**4.01.** As used in this Plan of Operation:

    **(a)** **"Board"** means the Board of Directors of the Association.

    **(b)** **"Commissioner"** means the Commissioner of the Office of Financial and Insurance Services of the State of Michigan or such person as may succeed the Commissioner in the regulation of insurance in the State of Michigan.

    **(c)** **"Michigan Insurance Code"** means the Michigan Insurance Code of 1956, as amended, as in force at the effective date of this Plan of Operation and as such law may thereafter be amended from time to time.

18

(d)    **"Member"** means (i) each insurer engaged in writing insurance coverages under policies of insurance providing the security required by Section 3101(1) of the Michigan Insurance Code for the owners and registrants of motor vehicles required to be registered in the State of Michigan, and (ii) each group self-insurance pool providing motor vehicle security under Section 9 of Act No. 138 of the Public Acts of 1982, being Section 124.9 of the Michigan Compiled Laws. If two or more such insurers are "affiliated" as that term is defined in Section 1301 of the Michigan Insurance Code, then such insurers shall be deemed to constitute and be one Member of the Association for all purposes of this Plan of Operation except where the context indicates otherwise. The term "Member" does not include 3103 Members.

(e)    **"3103 Member"** means each insurer engaged in writing insurance coverages under policies of insurance providing the security required by Section 3103(1) of the Michigan Insurance Code for the owners and registrants of motorcycles required to be registered in the State of Michigan. If two or more such insurers are "affiliated" as that term is defined in Section 1301 of the Michigan Insurance Code, then such insurers shall be deemed to constitute and be one 3103 Member of the Association for all purposes of this Plan of Operation except where the context indicates otherwise.

(f)    **"Earned Car Years"** means the number of earned vehicle years (or the total number of earned vehicle months divided by twelve, if so reported) of insurance providing to any and all vehicles the security required by Sections 3101 and 3103 of the Michigan Insurance Code, written in the State of Michigan by each Member and 3103 Member, or all such members, as applicable. As used in the term "Earned Car Years" and in this definition, "car" includes motorcycle. The Board may establish, by resolution, the manner for determining Earned Car Years with respect to commercial or other vehicles where some other unit of exposure is used.

(g)    **"Historical Vehicle"** means a vehicle that is a registered historic vehicle under section 803A or 803P of the Michigan Vehicle Code, 1949 PA 300 MCL 257.803A and 257.803P.

(h)    **"Written Car Years"** means the number of net direct written vehicle years (or the total number of net direct written vehicle months divided by twelve, if so reported) of insurance providing to any and all vehicles, except Historical Vehicles, the security required by Sections 3101 and 3103 of the Michigan Insurance Code, written in the State of Michigan by each Member and 3103 Member, or all such members, as applicable. The method each Member and 3103 Member uses to calculate Written Car Years for the purpose of reporting such information to the Association shall be the same method the member uses to calculate the number of written car years the member reports to its statistical agent. As used in the term "Written Car Years" and in this definition, "car" includes motorcycle. The Board may establish, by resolution, the manner for determining Written Car Years with respect to commercial or other vehicles where some other unit of exposure is used.

(i)    **"Written Historical Vehicle Years"** means the number of net direct written Historical Vehicle years (or the total number of net direct written Historical Vehicle months divided by twelve, if so reported) of insurance providing to any and all Historical Vehicles the security required by Sections 3101 and 3103 of the Michigan Insurance Code, written in the State of Michigan by each Member and 3103 Member, or all such members, as applicable. The method each Member and 3103 Member uses to calculate Written Historical Vehicle Years for the purpose of reporting such information to the Association shall be the same method the member uses to calculate the number of Written Car Years the member reports to its statistical agent, except that this method will be applied to policies on Historical Vehicles.

(j)    **"Reimbursable Ultimate Loss"** means the actual loss payments (exclusive of optional wage loss payments and of wage loss, medical, hospital and related costs not required to be paid by a Member because of the coordination of benefits) in excess of the applicable amount set forth in section 3104(2) of the Michigan Insurance Code, sustained under personal protection insurance coverages under policies of insurance providing the security required by section 3101(1) of the Michigan Insurance Code for the owners and registrants of motor vehicles required to be registered in the State of Michigan, which a Member is obligated to

REV. 06/16/03, eff. 7/1/03

pay by reason of an occurrence and which are paid or payable by the Member. For purposes of determining the amount applicable under section 3104(2), a policy of insurance is considered to be issued or renewed on the date the policy (or renewal, as the case may be) becomes effective. If a Member is obligated to pay such loss amounts to two or more claimants under one or more policies of insurance by reason of a single occurrence, the "Reimbursable Ultimate Loss" shall be the amount by which the aggregate of such actual loss payments exceed the applicable amount set forth in section 3104(2) of the Michigan Insurance Code (except as set forth in the next sentence). "Reimbursable Ultimate Loss" includes losses paid or payable on policies written by a Member on behalf of the Michigan Automobile Insurance Placement Facility, but losses payable under such a policy having an effective date on or after January 1, 1981, shall not be aggregated with losses under any similar policies or with losses under any other policy for purposes of determining the "Reimbursable Ultimate Loss" sustained by the Member. "Reimbursable Ultimate Loss" shall not include loss adjustment, investigating service or legal fees (except as otherwise provided in Section 10.06 of this Plan) or any other claim expenses; nor interest or court costs; nor exemplary or punitive damages; nor any amounts payable under the provisions of the Uniform Trade Practices Act, MCLA 500.2001 et seq., (as presently in force or hereafter amended), or similar provisions of law in another jurisdiction; nor any amounts payable for refusal by a Member to pay amounts due under a policy of insurance (unless the Association previously has specifically approved in writing the action taken by the Member out of which the claim arises).

## ARTICLE V
### Membership

**5.01. Membership.** Every insurer who, by virtue of the provisions of Section 3104(1) of the Michigan Insurance Code, as amended, is required to be a member of the Association as a condition of its authority to transact insurance in the State of Michigan, shall be a Member. (Notwithstanding the foregoing, the Assigned Claims Facility and Plan created pursuant to Section 3171 of the Michigan Insurance Code, shall not be a member of the Association.) Every group self-insurance pool providing motor vehicle security under Section 9 of Act No. 138 of the Public Acts of 1982, shall be a Member.

**5.02. 3103 Membership.** Every insurer who, by virtue of the provisions of Section 3103(1) of the Michigan Insurance Code, as amended, is required to be a member of the Association for assessment purposes as a condition of its authority to transact insurance in the State of Michigan, shall be a 3103 Member.

**5.03. Withdrawal.** An insurer may withdraw as a Member or 3103 Member of the Association upon ceasing to write insurance which provides the security required by Section 3101 or Section 3103 in the State of Michigan, provided that (i) such withdrawal shall be effective as of the day following the day on which the insurer's premium obligation is finally determined for the Association's fiscal year during which the insurer ceased to provide such insurance within the State of Michigan, (ii) all unpaid premiums and interest which have been charged to the withdrawing insurer shall be due and payable as of the effective date of the withdrawal, and (iii) the withdrawing insurer shall continue to be bound by the Plan of Operation with respect to the performance and completion of any unsatisfied liabilities and obligations (including the continuing obligation to submit reports regarding claims pursuant to Section 10.01) to the Association. A group self-insurance pool may withdraw as a Member of the Association upon ceasing to provide motor vehicle security, provided that (i) such withdrawal shall be effective as of the day following the day on which the pool's premium obligation is finally determined for the Association's fiscal year during which the pool ceased to provide such security within the State of Michigan, (ii) all unpaid premiums and interest which have been charged to the withdrawing pool shall be due and payable as of the effective date of the withdrawal, and (iii) the withdrawing pool and its members shall continue to be bound by the Plan of Operation with respect to the performance and completion of any unsatisfied liabilities and obligations (including the continuing obligation to submit reports regarding claims pursuant to Section 10.01) to the Association.

**5.04. Merger.** When a Member or 3103 Member has been merged or consolidated into another insurer or another insurer has reinsured such a member's entire business which provide the security required by Section

3101 or Section 3103 in this State, the member and the insurer which is the successor in interest of the member shall be liable for the member's obligations to the Association. When a member group self-insurance pool has been merged or consolidated into another pool which provides the security required by law, the member pool and the pool which is its successor in interest shall be liable for all the former's obligations to the Association.

**5.05. Michigan Automobile Insurance Placement Facility.** As used in this Plan of Operation, "policies written on behalf of the Michigan Automobile Insurance Placement Facility" means policies of insurance issued by a Member pursuant to a loss sharing plan as authorized by Sections 3320(1)(c) and 3330(1) (e) of the Insurance Code. Except as otherwise provided herein, policies written by a Member on behalf of the Michigan Automobile Insurance Placement Facility (hereinafter "MAIPF") shall be treated in the same manner as any other policy written by that member. Policies written by a Member under a special risk distribution procedure as authorized by Section 3320 (1) (a) of the Insurance Code shall be treated in the same manner as policies issued by the Member as voluntary business (including for purposes of aggregation under Section 4.01 (f)).

## ARTICLE VI
### Board of Directors

**6.01. Powers.** The Board of Directors shall have responsibility for the administration of the Plan and the management of the affairs and operation of the Association, consistent with the Plan of Operation and the provisions of the Michigan Insurance Code.

**6.02. Numbers, Selection and Qualifications.** The Board of Directors shall consist of five (5) Members, each of whom shall be appointed by the Commissioner pursuant to Section 3104(11) of the Insurance Code.

**6.03. Term.** A director shall hold office for the term for which appointed and until the successor shall have been appointed and qualified, or until resignation. All Directors appointed to serve terms (other than a vacancy) will be appointed for a four year term.

**6.04. Ex Officio Member of the Board.** The Commissioner, or a representative designated by the Commissioner, shall be an ex officio member of the Board without vote (but shall not be counted for purposes of determining if a quorum is present).

**6.05. Resignations; Vacancies.** The resignation of a director is effective upon receipt by the Association of written notice thereof or at such subsequent time as is set forth in the notice of resignation. Any vacancy in the Board of Directors shall be filled by appointment by the Commissioner, and the Member so appointed shall hold office for the unexpired term in respect of which such vacancy occurred.

**6.06. Appointment of Designated Representatives.** Each member of the Board shall select a qualified person as its designated representative who shall act for such member in all matters, including attendance and voting at all meetings of the Board. In the event of the absence of the designated representative from any meeting, the member shall appoint a substitute representative who may attend with like powers in the designated representative's place and stead.

**6.07. Reimbursement for Expenses.** Members of the Board shall serve without compensation, but they may be reimbursed, to the extent and in the manner approved by the Board, for their actual and necessary expenses incurred in attendance at Board meetings, committee meetings or otherwise in connection with Association business. The Board may authorize reimbursement of the actual and necessary expenses incurred by others in serving on committees established by the Board or otherwise assisting the Board in the performance of its duties.

## ARTICLE VII
### Meetings of Board of Directors

**7.01. Quorum and Votes.** At any meeting of the Board of Directors, four (4) members of the Board shall constitute a quorum for the transaction of business, and the acts of a majority of the Directors present at a meeting at which a quorum is present shall be the acts of the Board. Each member of the Board shall have one vote, and the Chair shall retain the right to vote on all issues.

**7.02. Annual Meeting.** A regular annual meeting of the Board of Directors shall be held at such time as is designated by the Board. The annual meeting shall be held at the office of the Association or at such other place within the State of Michigan as is designated by the Board. At each annual meeting or at a special meeting held pursuant to Section 7.03, the Board shall:

    (1)    Review the Plan of Operation and determine if any changes are necessary.

    (2)    Review each outstanding contract and determine if any changes are necessary.

    (3)    Review the premium charges and determine the adequacy thereof.

    (4)    Review the arrangements with any custodian bank or trust company.

    (5)    Review the adequacy of the reports, information and statistics submitted by Members and 3103 Members and determine any necessary improvements or action.

    (6)    Receive and consider reports from the standing committees and other committees.

    (7)    Discuss and consider such other matters as may be appropriate.

**7.03. Special Meetings.** Special meetings of the Board of Directors may be called by or at the request of the Chair, the Commissioner, or any three members of the Board. Directors shall be notified of any special meeting of the Board at least three (3) days in advance of the meeting, and such notice shall state the time, place and purpose of the meeting. Any Director may waive notice of any meeting.

**7.04. Participation by Telephonic Means.** A member of the Board of Directors may participate in any meeting of the Board by means of conference telephone or similar communications equipment by means of which all persons participating in the meeting may hear and otherwise communicate with each other. Participation in a meeting pursuant to this section constitutes presence in person at the meeting. In addition to the foregoing, members of the Board may vote by telephone and a unanimous affirmative vote of the Board taken by a telephone poll shall be deemed the same as action taken at a Board meeting at which a quorum was present.

**7.05. Written Consent.** Any action required or permitted at any meeting of the Board, may be taken without a meeting, without prior notice, and without a vote, if all of the Directors consent thereto in writing.

## ARTICLE VIII
### Officers

**8.01.** The Board of Directors shall elect a Chair, and may elect a Vice-Chair, at its annual meeting, and may elect such other officers from time to time as it shall deem desirable.

(a)    The Chair shall preside at all meetings of the Board of Directors. The Chair may sign any deeds, mortgages, bonds, contracts or other instruments which the Board of Directors has authorized to be executed. The Chair shall discharge such other duties as may be incidental to the office or as shall be prescribed by the Board of Directors from time to time. The Chair shall serve as an ex officio member of all committees.

(b)    In the absence of the Chair, the Vice-Chair, if one is elected, shall perform the duties of the Chair.

## ARTICLE IX
### Premiums

**9.01.    Calculation of Premiums**. The Board shall determine the Total Premium, the Average Total Premium Per Car and Historical Vehicle, the Average Premium Per Car, and the Average Premium Per Historical Vehicle prior to or at the earliest practicable time during the period for which the premium is applicable.

(a)    The Board shall calculate a **"Total Premium"** sufficient to cover the expected losses (including incurred but not reported losses for the period), charges payable to reinsurers under reinsurance agreements, and expenses of the Association (including any costs or expenses of indemnification payable pursuant to Article XVIII) which the Association will likely incur during each annual (or other) period for which the premium is applicable. In addition to the method described in section 9.08 for the return of surplus to Members and 3103 Members, the total premium may be adjusted for any excess or deficiency in premiums from previous periods and, at the discretion of the Board, any such excesses or deficiencies may be fully adjusted in a single period or may be adjusted over several periods ratably or in such proportion as the Board may deem advisable.

(b)    An **"Average Total Premium Per Car and Historical Vehicle"** is calculated by dividing the Total Premium determined pursuant to section 9.01.(a) by the sum of the estimated total Written Car Years of all Members and 3103 Members during the period to which the premium applies and 100% of the Written Historical Vehicle Years of all members and 3103 Members during the period to which the premium applies.

(c)    An **"Average Premium Per Car"** is calculated by dividing the total premium determined pursuant to section 9.01.(a) by the sum of the estimated total Written Car Years of all Members and 3103 Members during the period to which the premium applies and 20% of the Written Historical Vehicle Years of all members and 3103 Members during the period to which the premium applies.

(d)    An **"Average Premium Per Historical Vehicle"** is calculated by multiplying the Average Premium Per Car as determined pursuant to section 9.01.(c) by 20%.

**9.02.    Preliminary Premium Assessment.** The Association shall charge to each Member and 3103 Member, prior to or at the earliest practicable time during the period for which the premium is applicable, a preliminary premium assessment to be calculated as follows:

(a)     For the annual period beginning July 1, 2002, the preliminary premium assessment for each Member and 3103 Member shall be an amount equal to such member's total Earned Car Years written during the 2001 calendar year, multiplied by the Average Premium Per Car for the annual period beginning July 1, 2002.

(b)     For annual (or other periodic) premium assessment periods beginning on or after July 1, 2003, the preliminary premium assessment for each Member and 3103 Member shall be an amount equal to the sum of (i) such member's total Written Car Years during the immediately preceding assessment period (or such other annualized period as the Board may select), multiplied by the Average Premium Per Car for the current assessment period, and (ii) such member's total Written Historical Vehicle Years during the immediately preceding assessment period (or such other annualized period as the Board may select), multiplied by the Average Premium Per Historical Vehicle for the current assessment period.

The preliminary premium shall be allocated among and charged to Members and 3103 Members on such periodic basis as the Board may establish. The periodic charges need not be uniform in amount.

**9.03. Final Premium Assessment.** As soon as is practicable after the end of each annual (or other) period for which the premium is applicable, the Association shall charge to each Member and 3103 Member a final premium assessment for the period just completed. The final premium payable by each Member and 3103 Member will be determined as follows:

(a)     For the annual premium assessment period beginning July 1, 2002, the final premium assessment for each Member and 3103 Member shall be an amount equal to such member's total Written Car Years and Written Historical Vehicle Years during such period, multiplied by the Average Total Premium Per Car and Historical Vehicle for the period.

(b)     For annual (or other periodic) premium assessment periods beginning on or after July 1, 2003, the final premium assessment for each Member and 3103 Member shall be an amount equal to the sum of (i) such member's total Written Car Years during such period, multiplied by the Average Premium Per Car for the period, and (ii) such member's total Written Historical Vehicle Years during such period multiplied by the Average Premium Per Historical Vehicle for the period.

**9.04. Application of Prior Premium Payments.** Any payments made by a Member or 3103 Member pursuant to Section 9.02 will be applied against the premium ultimately payable for the completed period pursuant to Section 9.03 and each Member and 3103 Member will be charged for any deficiency or credited for any excess (such credit, at the option of the Board, to be applied against premiums subsequently due pursuant to Sections 9.02 and 9.03 or refunded to the Member or 3103 Member).

**9.05. Payment.** Premiums charged under Sections 9.02 and 9.03 shall be paid by Members and 3103 Members in full within such period of time after the premium charge is billed by the Association as the Board may establish. The Association shall have the right to audit and verify any Member's or 3103 Member's determination of a premium payable under this Article IX. In connection with any such audit, a Member or 3103 Member shall provide such documentation supporting its determination of the premium payable as the Association may request.

**9.06. Policies on Behalf of MAIPF.** Any Member who writes policies on behalf of the MAIPF is ultimately liable for premiums based upon car years so written; nevertheless, that portion of a Member's premium that is based upon policies written on behalf of MAIPF may be billed to and paid by either the Member or MAIPF for the account of the Member.

**9.07. Allocation of Liabilities.** The Board shall establish, by resolution, the method for redistributing subsequently determined excesses or deficiencies in the premium assessment for a particular period. In any dispute as to the method to be used, the determination of the Board shall be final and the Member or 3103 Member shall be bound thereby.

**9.08. Lump Sum Distribution of Surplus.** At the discretion of the Board, excesses in premiums from previous periods may be adjusted at any time by way of a lump sum distribution of surplus to Members and 3103 Members. In the event the Board determines to adjust excesses in such manner, the distribution to each Member and 3103 Member shall be calculated in a manner determined by the Board. Without limiting the means available to the Board under the preceding sentence for calculating the distribution, the Board may base the amount of the distribution to each Member and 3103 Member on the sum total of (a) the number of vehicles subject to a premium assessment by the association for which the security required by section 3101(1) or 3103(1) of the Michigan Insurance Code is in effect as of a date specified by the Board by resolution, and (b) the number of vehicles subject to a premium assessment by the association for which the security required by section 3101(1) or 3103(1) of the Michigan Insurance Code is not in effect as of the specified date, but for which comprehensive and/or collision coverage is in effect as of the specified date and the security otherwise required by section 3101(1) or 3103(1) of the Michigan Insurance Code is not required because the vehicle is not being "driven or moved upon a highway" as that term is used in section 3101(1) of the Michigan Insurance Code.

## ARTICLE X
### Operations

**10.01. Reports Regarding Claims.** Members and 3103 Members shall report to the Association such information as the Board may require on forms prescribed by the Board: (a) As soon as practicable after the loss occurrence, Members shall report each claim which, on the basis of the injuries or damages sustained, may reasonably be anticipated to result in a Reimbursable Ultimate Loss, and for purposes of reporting the Member shall consider itself legally liable for the injuries and damages. (The Board may specify, in its discretion, the types of injuries and/or amounts of claims which must be reported to the Association); (b) Promptly, or on such periodic basis as the Board may prescribe, Members shall report any changes in the amount of the reserve established with respect to any such claim or of any subsequent developments likely to materially affect the interest of the Association in the claim; (c) At such times as the Board may fix, Members shall report such loss and expense data, statistics and other information as the Board may require; (d) The MAIPF shall promptly notify the Association when a Member ceases to be authorized to write policies on behalf of MAIPF. Such a Member is not relieved of its responsibility for providing the Association with all usual or necessary reports regarding claims arising from policies it wrote on behalf of MAIPF, unless MAIPF assigns this responsibility to another Member.

**10.02. Inadequate or Untimely Reports.** If a Member or 3103 Member refuses to timely submit the reports or information required of it pursuant to Section 10.01 or otherwise, or if the Board should determine that the reports and information submitted by a Member or 3103 Member are unreliable or incomplete, the Board may, at the member's expense, direct that an authorized representative of the Association (which may be another member) shall audit and inspect such member's records and compile the required information and data.

**10.03. Association's Data.** The Association shall maintain such loss and expense data as to its liabilities as the Board deems appropriate and necessary.

**10.04. Reimbursement.** The Association shall reimburse each Member for 100% of the Reimbursable Ultimate Loss sustained by such Member resulting from a loss attributable to an accident which occurs on or after July 1, 1978. The Association shall also reimburse each insurer and group self-insurance pool (who shall be deemed to be a "Member" for purposes of Articles X and XI) who has withdrawn as a Member of the Association, or who has succeeded to the obligations of a former member by way of merger or consolidation, for 100% of the Reimbursable Ultimate Loss sustained by such former member, insurer or pool, as the case may be, resulting from a loss attributable to an accident which occurs on or after July 1, 1978.

**10.05. Reimbursement Payments.** With respect to any claim which involves a Reimbursable Ultimate Loss, the Member shall submit to the Association an itemized account, on such forms and with such supporting documentation of claims payments as the Board may prescribe, as soon as practicable after the close of the fiscal quarter for which reimbursement is sought. A Member may elect reimbursement on a monthly basis if its surplus is $10 million or less as shown on the most recent annual statement on file with the commissioner of insurance at the time the request for reimbursement is made. The Association shall, upon verification of the propriety and amount of the payments made and the Member's entitlement to reimbursement therefor, reimburse the Member the amount due it. Any Reimbursable Ultimate Loss arising under a policy issued by a Member on behalf of the MAIPF, may be paid directly to the Member or to MAIPF for the account of the Member. If responsibility for making payments under such a policy is transferred from one Member to another by MAIPF, reimbursement of loss payments made under that policy will be as directed by MAIPF.

**10.06. Recovery from Other Sources.** Whenever a Member recovers from a third party an amount for which it has already been reimbursed by the Association, the Member shall promptly turn such recovered monies over to the Association to the extent of any reimbursement theretofore received, provided that the Board may permit a Member to retain therefrom such amount as the Board deems reasonable and necessary attorney fees and litigation costs incurred in connection with obtaining the recovery from the third party.

**10.07. Review of Claims Procedures and Practices.** The Association shall have the right, on the giving of reasonable notice, to review through its authorized representative (which may be another member) the claims procedures and practices of any member and to audit and inspect.

**10.08. Inadequate Claims Procedures and Practices.** If, in the judgment of the Board, the claims procedures or practices of a member are inadequate to properly service the liabilities of the Association or jeopardize the interests of the Association, the Association may, at the member's expense, undertake or contract with another person (including another member) to adjust, or assist in the adjustment of, claims for the member which create a potential liability to the Association.

## ARTICLE XI
### Defaults

**11.01. Interest Charges.** If any Member or 3103 Member fails to timely pay the premium or interest charged to it, interest shall be charged the Member or 3103 Member on all past due amounts or deficiencies at such rate as the Board may establish from time to time.

**11.02. Other Action.** If any Member or 3103 Member fails to timely pay the premium or interest charged to it, and such deficiency is not cured within ten (10) days after notice in writing thereof is sent by the Association to the delinquent member, the Association may, at the discretion of the Board, offset the past due amount or deficiency against any reimbursement payment then or thereafter payable to Member or 3103 Member under Section 10.05 for the purpose of satisfying in full the liabilities and obligations of the Member or 3103 Member to the Association. The Board may also authorize the taking of such other action as it deems proper and appropriate, including the institution of legal action or invoking the assistance of the Commissioner with respect to such action as may be permitted under the Michigan Insurance Code. Any legal and other expenses incurred by the Association as the result of a Member's or 3103 Member's default, shall be charged to and paid by the Member or 3103 Member.

## ARTICLE XII
### Insolvency of a Member

**12.01. Apportionment of Liability Among Members.** If a domiciliary receiver is appointed for a present or former Member or a present or former 3103 Member for purposes of liquidation, any liability of such insurer
REV. 06/16/03, eff. 7/1/03

left unsatisfied shall be apportioned among the remaining members of the Association in proportion to the premium charges made by the Association (exclusive of any premium charged the insolvent insurer) pursuant to Section 9.03 for the period within which the receiver was appointed by the final order of a court having jurisdiction over such insolvent insurer. The unsatisfied liability of the insolvent insurer so apportioned among the members of the Association, shall be part of the premium payable by such members pursuant to Section 9.03.

**12.02.  Apportionment of Recovery.**  The Association shall have, on behalf of all of the remaining members, all rights allowed by law against the estate or funds of the insolvent Member or 3103 Member for sums due the Association, and any amounts received by the Association as a result thereof shall be credited to the members in proportion to the share of the insolvent insurer's liability theretofore charged to them pursuant to Section 12.01.  At the discretion of the Board, such credits may be handled in the manner described in Section 9.04.

## ARTICLE XIII
### Administration

**13.01.  Address.**  The official address of the Association shall be the address of the Association=s administrative office unless otherwise designated by the Board.

**13.02.  Performance of Administrative Functions.**  The Board may employ such persons, firms or corporations as it deems appropriate to perform the administrative functions necessary for the performance of any of the duties imposed on the Board or the Association.  The Board may use the mailing address of such person, firm or corporation as the official office address of the Association.  Such person, firm or corporation shall keep such records of its activities as may be required by the Board.

**13.03.  Bank Accounts.**  The Board may open bank accounts for use in Association business.  Reasonable delegation of deposit and withdrawal authority to such accounts for Association business may be made consistent with prudent fiscal policy.

**13.04.  Borrowings.**  The Board may borrow money from any person or organization, including a member insurer, as the Board in its judgment deems advantageous for the Association.

**13.05.  Reinsurance.**  The Board may reinsure all or any portion of the potential liability of the Association, with reinsurers licensed to transact insurance in Michigan or approved by the Commissioner.  The Board may contract with such reinsurer(s) to perform any of the activities of the Association referred to in Article X and any other administrative functions of the Association.

**13.06.  Office, etc.**  The Board may purchase or lease such housing and equipment, and may employ such personnel, as it deems necessary to assure the efficient operation of the Association.

**13.07.  Contracting with Others.**  The Board may contract with one or more persons, firms or corporations (including a member) for such goods and services as may be required to carry out the efficient operation of the Association, including claims management, actuarial services, investment services and legal services.

**13.08.  Investments.**  All monies due the Association for premiums or interest shall be paid to the Association and held, disbursed, invested and reinvested, and securities acquired by investment of the Association's cash funds or otherwise may be disposed of, by the Board in accordance with this Plan of Operation and such resolutions and rules as may be adopted by the Board, provided, however, that investments made hereunder shall only be such as may be made by domestic casualty companies under the Michigan Insurance Code and known as capital and reserve investments.

27

**13.09. Income on Association's Assets.** All profit or loss arising from the investment of funds held by the Association, and all income from such investment of funds, shall be added to and become a part of, during the period realized or received by the Association, the general funds of the Association and may be used for the purpose of paying expenses of the Association and Reimbursable Ultimate Losses.

**13.10. Adoption of Rules, etc.** The Board may adopt reasonable rules and policies for the administration of the Association, enforce such, and delegate authority, as the Board considers necessary to assure the proper administration and operation of the Association consistent with this Plan of Operation.

### ARTICLE XIV
#### Committees

**14.01. Standing Committees.** The Chair of the Board shall appoint standing committees (which may, but need not, consist of members of the Association) as follows:

**a)** An Actuarial Committee which shall make recommendations to the Board regarding the premium charges for each period and report to the Board regarding the sufficiency of prior premium charges.

**(b)** An Investment Committee, which shall establish the investment policy of the Association, subject to such guidelines as may be established in this Plan of Operation and by the Board.

**(c)** A Claims Committee, which shall review claims procedures and practices of member companies, generally or with respect to specific cases, pursuant to procedures approved by the Board, and make recommendations to the Board, and take such action as may be deemed proper pursuant to Article X.

**(d)** An Audit Committee, which shall, itself or through a designated representative, review and audit the books and records of the Association and report to the Board on the financial condition of the Association.

**14.02. Other Committees.** The Chair may appoint such other standing committees or special committees as may be deemed necessary for the transaction of business and conduct of affairs.

### ARTICLE XV
#### Complaints and Appeals

**15.01.** Any Member or 3103 Member or other interested person aggrieved with respect to any action or decision of the Board or the Association, or any committee or representative thereof, may within thirty (30) days file a complaint with the Board of Directors concerning such. The Board, or a committee appointed by it, shall hear and render a determination upon the complaint within a reasonable length of time after receipt thereof.

## ARTICLE XVI
### Records and Reports

**16.01. Minutes.** A written record of the important proceedings of each Board meeting shall be made. The original of this record shall be retained by the Chair, with copies furnished to each Board member.

**16.02. Annual Reports.** The Board shall make an annual report to the Commissioner and to each Member and 3103 Member. Such report shall include a review of the Association's transactions, activities and affairs and an accounting of its income and disbursements for the past year.

**16.03. Examination of Records, etc.** The books of account, records, reports and other documents of the Association shall be open to inspection by Members and 3103 Members only at such times and under such conditions and regulations as the Board shall reasonably determine. Claim, underwriting and other nonpublic information relating to any specific risk, claimant, plaintiff or defendant shall be treated as confidential by the Association and will not be disclosed unless the Association is legally required or permitted to do so.

## ARTICLE XVII
### Fiscal Year

**17.01.** The fiscal year of the Association shall begin on the first day of July and end on the last day of June of each year, or on such other dates as the Board may determine by a duly adopted resolution.

## ARTICLE XVIII
### Limitation of Liability and Indemnification

**18.01. Limitation of Liability.** A director is not personally liable to the Association or its Members and 3103 Members for monetary damages for a breach of the director's fiduciary duty except for (i) a breach of the director's duty of loyalty to the Association or its Members and 3103 Members, (ii) acts or omissions not in good faith of that involve intentional misconduct or knowing violation of law, (iii) a transaction from which the director derived an improper personal benefit or (iv) acts or omissions occurring before January 1, 1989.

**18.02. Non-Derivative Actions.** Subject to all of the other provisions of this Article XVIII, the Association shall indemnify any person who was or is a party or is threatened to be made a party to any threatened, pending or completed action, suit or proceeding, whether civil, criminal, administrative or investigative and whether formal or informal, other than an action by or in the right of the Association, by reason of the fact that the person is or was a director or officer of the Association, including a member of any committee or subcommittee of the Association, against expenses, including attorneys' fees, judgments, penalties, fines, and amounts paid in settlement actually and reasonably incurred by him or her in connection with such action, suit or proceeding if the person acted in good faith and in a manner the person reasonably believed to be in or not opposed to the best interests of the Association or its members, and with respect to any criminal action or proceeding, if the person had no reasonable cause to believe his or her conduct was unlawful. The termination of any action, suit or proceeding by judgment, order, settlement, conviction, or upon a plea of nolo contendere or its equivalent, shall not, of itself, create a presumption that the person did not act in good faith and in a manner which the person reasonably believed to be in or not opposed to the best interests of the Association or its members, and, with respect to any criminal action or proceeding, had reasonable cause to believe that his or her conduct was unlawful.

**18.03. Derivative Actions.** Subjects to all of the provisions of this Article XVIII, the Association shall indemnify any person who was or is a party to or is threatened to be made a party to any threatened, pending or completed action or suit by or in the right of the Association to procure a judgment in its favor by reason of the fact that the person is or was a director or officer of the Association, including a member of any committee or subcommittee of the Association, against expenses, including actual and reasonable attorneys' fees, and amounts paid in settlement incurred by the person in connection with such action or suit if the person acted in good faith and in a manner the person reasonably believed to be in or not opposed to the best interests of the Association or its members. However, indemnification shall not be made for any claim, issue or matter in which such person has been found liable to the Association unless and only to the extent that the court in which such action or suit was brought has determined upon application that, despite the adjudication of liability but in view of all circumstances of the case, such person is fairly and reasonably entitled to indemnification for the expenses which the court considers proper.

**18.04.  Expenses of Successful Defense.**  To the extent that a person entitled to indemnification has been successful on the merits or otherwise in defense of any action, suit or proceeding referred to in Sections 18.02 or 18.03 above, or in defense of any claim, issue or matter in the action, suit or proceeding, the person shall be indemnified against expenses, including actual and reasonable attorneys' fees, incurred by such person in connection with the action, suit or proceeding and any action , suit, or proceeding brought to enforce the mandatory indemnification provided by this Section 18.04.

**18.05.  Contract Right; Limitation on Indemnity.**  The right to indemnification conferred in this Article XVIII shall be a contract right, and shall apply to services of a director or officer as an employee or agent of the Association as well as in such person's capacity as a director or officer.  Except as provided in section 18.04 above, the Association shall have no obligations under this Article XVIII to indemnify any person in connection with any proceeding, or part thereof, initiated by such person without authorization by the Board.

**18.06.  Determination That Indemnification is Proper.**  Any indemnification under Section 18.02 and 18.03 above (unless ordered by a court) shall be made by the Association only as authorized in the specific case upon a determination that indemnification of the person is proper in the circumstances because the person has met the applicable standard of conduct set forth in Sections 18.02 and 18.03, whichever is applicable. Such determination and evaluation shall be made in any of the following ways:

(1)     By a majority vote of a quorum of the Board consisting of directors who were not parties to the action, suit or proceeding.

(2)     If the quorum described in clause (1) above is not obtainable, then by a majority vote of a committee of directors duly designated by the Board who are not parties (or whose individual representatives were not parties) to the action.  The committee shall consist of not less than two (2) disinterested directors.

(3)     By independent legal counsel in a written opinion.

(4)     By vote of the members.

**18.07.  Proportionate Indemnity.**  If a person is entitled to indemnification under Sections 18.02 and 18.03 above for a portion of expenses, including attorneys' fees, judgments, penalties, fines and amounts paid in settlement, but not for the total amount thereof, the Association shall indemnify the person for the portion of the expenses, judgments, penalties, fines, or amounts paid in settlement for which the person is entitled to be indemnified.

**18.08   Expense Advance.**  The Association may pay or reimburse the expenses incurred by a person referred to in Sections 18.02 and 18.03 above who is a party or threatened to be made a party to an action, suit, or proceeding in advance of final disposition of the proceeding upon receipt of an undertaking by or on behalf of such person to repay the expenses if it is ultimately determined that such person is not entitled to be indemnified by the Association.  The undertaking shall be by unlimited general obligation of the person on whose behalf advances are made but need not be secured.

**18.09. Non-Exclusivity of Rights.** The indemnification or advancement of expenses provided under this Article XVIII is not exclusive of other rights to which a person seeking indemnification or advancement of expenses may be entitled under a contractual arrangement with the Association. However, the total amount of expenses advanced or indemnified from all sources combined shall not exceed the amount of actual expenses incurred by the person seeking indemnification or advancement of expenses.

**18.10. Former Directors and Officers.** The indemnification provided in this Article XVIII continues as to a person who has ceased to be a director or officer and as to any other person entitled to indemnification who has ceased to hold the position creating such entitlement, and shall inure to the benefit of the heirs, executors and administrators of such person.

**18.11. Definition of Director, Etc.** For purpose of this Article XVIII, director, officer and committee or sub-committee member shall be deemed to include both the insurer designated, appointed or serving in that capacity and any individual designated by the insurer to act or serve as its representative, and the word "person" shall be deemed to include any such insurer.

**18.12. Indemnification of Employees and agents of the Association.** The Association may, to the extent authorized from time to time by the Board, grant rights to indemnification and to the advancement of expenses to any employee or agent of the Association to the fullest extent of the provisions of this Article XVIII with respect to the indemnification and advancement of expenses of directors and officers of the Association.

**18.13. Changes in Michigan Law.** In the event of any change of the Michigan statutory provisions applicable to the Association relating to the subject matter of this Article XVIII, then the indemnification to which any person shall be entitled hereunder shall be determined by such changed provisions, but only to the extent that any such change permits the Association to provide broader indemnification rights than such provisions permitted the Association to provide prior to any such change. Subject to Section 18.14 below, the Board is authorized to amend this Article XVIII to conform to any such changed statutory provisions.

**18.14. Amendment or Repeal of Article XVIII.** No amendment or repeal of this Article XVIII shall apply to or have any effect on any director or officer of the Association for or with respect to any acts or omissions of such director or officer occurring prior to such amendment or repeal.

**18.15. Treatment of Expenses.** The expense of any indemnification or reimbursement shall be treated as a cost of administering the Association in the year in which payment is made by the Association and shall be assessed among and paid by all Members and 3103 Members in the manner provided in Article IX.

## ARTICLE XIX
### Mail Ballot by Members

**19.01.** Any matter, including the amendment of this Plan of Operation, upon which the members are required or permitted to vote, may be submitted to the Members and voted upon by them by mail. The Board shall fix a date for the counting of votes on proposals submitted to Members by mail, and such proposals shall be mailed to the Members for voting not less than fifteen (15) days prior to the date fixed by the Board for the counting of the votes.

**19.02.** Each Member shall be allotted the number of votes equal to the number of its total Written Car Years during the most recent annualized period for which such information is available. In the event Written Car Year data for all Members is not yet available to the Association, each Member shall be allotted the number of votes equal to the number of its total Earned Car Years written during the most recent annualized period for which such information is available. Unless otherwise provided herein, a proposal submitted to the Members for a vote by mail shall be adopted if approved by a majority of the total number of votes which Members are entitled to cast as of the date the votes are counted.

## ARTICLE XX
### Conformity to Statute

**20.01.** Section 3104 of the Michigan Insurance Code (Act No. 136, P.A. 1978), as written, and as may be amended, is incorporated as part of this Plan of Operation.

## ARTICLE XXI
### Amendments

**21.01.** This Plan of Operation may be amended, altered or repealed, in whole or in part, (i) by majority vote of the Board of Directors; (ii) ratified by a majority vote of the Members, each Member being allotted the number of votes equal to the number of its total Written Car Years during the most recent annualized period for which such information is available (or, if Written Car Year data for all Members is not yet available to the Association, each Member being allotted the number of votes equal to the number of its total Earned Car Years written during the most recent annualized period for which such information is available); and (iii) with the approval of the Commissioner.

*The Educated Consumers Guide to No-Fault Automobile Insurance*

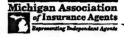 

**FOR IMMEDIATE RELEASE**          December 2, 2004
**Contact: Gary Mitchell (517) 323-9473**

## NATIONAL STUDY HAILS MICHIGAN'S NO-FAULT SYSTEM

(LANSING)— The Michigan Association of Insurance Agents today released a new study by the Insurance Research Council that finds insurance rates and claim losses lower in Michigan than in other no-fault auto insurance states. Between the years 1997 to 2002, the average amounts of personal injury protection (PIP) claimants as a result of accidents increased just 2 percent in Michigan, compared to 122 percent in Colorado, 60 percent in New York and 37 percent in Florida (see attachment).

The study also revealed a large discrepancy in medical treatment received by injured motorists in each state. More than 33 percent of the PIP claimants in Colorado, Florida and New York went to a chiropractor compared to only 13 percent in Michigan. Twenty-two percent of New York PIP claimants went to alternative medical and therapy professionals, while only 1 percent of those did so in the state of Michigan.

Not only did the number of medical claims vary in no-fault states, it was also the cost to consumers that varied drastically. Again, Michigan's No-Fault Insurance System proved to be a national leader in that category as well. The average per-visit for chiropractor in Florida was $254, compared to $125 in Michigan. The average total charged per claim by chiropractors was more than three times higher in Florida ($4,837) and Colorado ($4,804) than in Michigan ($1,522). In 2002 (the most recent figures available), from the Insurance Information Institute, the average auto insurance expenditure in Michigan ($839) was 13 percent lower than New York ($1,087), 8 percent lower than Colorado ($914), and 4 percent lower than Florida ($870).

— Continued —

 1141 Centennial Way • Lansing, Michigan 48917
*Mailing Address:* P.O. Box 80620 • Lansing, Michigan 48908-0620
*Office:* 517-323-9473 • *Fax:* 517-323-1629 • *E-mail:* bigim@michiganagent.org
*Web Site:* www.michiganagent.org

33

"This study proves that Michigan has the best No-Fault Insurance System in the nation," said Gary Mitchell, spokesman for the Michigan Association of Insurance Agents. "It's what our members have been telling consumers, legislators and reporters for a long time." Mitchell also said that Michigan is the only state in the nation to offer unlimited medical and rehabilitation services, yet maintains insurance rates close to the national average.

The Michigan Association of Insurance Agents is a statewide trade group that represents approximately 10,000 independent Insurance Agents and industry employees.

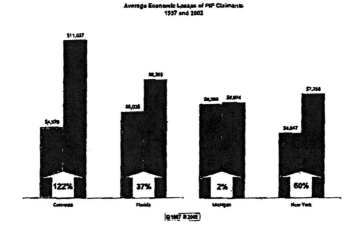

Average Economic Losses of PIP Claimants
1997 and 2002

Excludes permanent total disabilities, fatalities, and claimants with zero or missing economic loss.

*Note to editors: The Insurance Research Council is an independent, non-profit organization. This organization does not lobby or advocate legislative positions. For more detailed information on this study's methodology and findings, please contact Elizabeth Sprinkel at (610) 644-2212, Ext. 7568, or e-mail at irc@cpcuiia.org.*

Brought to you by the Southeastern
Michigan Domino's Pizza stores and The
Michigan Jaycee's!

• Spring is here! That means
cycling, skating and blading for
many. Protect your skull by
wearing a helmet every time!

• Traumatic Brain Injury (TBI) is
the leading cause of death and
disability in kids - but most
TBI's are preventable with the
use of a proper safety helmet.

*TBI Fact Sheets are available
by calling the Michigan
Jaycee's at 517-487-6077.*

*Hey Kids –Show us your SKULL SAFETY SMARTS! Just bring in this flyer and your
safety helmet and receive a free order of Domino's Breadsticks. Carryout only. One order
per customer. Offer good through September 2, 1996.*

## DOMINO'S PIZZA & MICHIGAN JAYCEE'S
## REMIND YOU TO ALWAYS WEAR A HELMET WHEN:

-BICYCLING     -SKATING OR BLADING     -SKATE BOARDING

• Domino's Pizza & the Michigan Jaycee's want to educate both parents
and children about the importance of wearing a helmet while skating,
cycling etc.

• Traumatic Brain Injury (TBI) is leading cause of death and disability in
children and young adults. *Most TBI's are preventable with the use of a
helmet.* Be a good role model and always wear a helmet!

*Interested in spreading the word about TBI prevention? TBI Fact Sheets are available by
calling the Michigan Jaycee's State Headquarters at 517-487-6077.*

DOMINO'S PIZZA & MICHIGAN JAYCEE'S

35

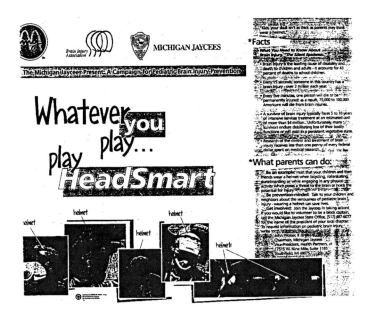

**Simkins & Simkins, P.C.**
*Attorneys at Law*

Charles N. Simkins
M. Martha Simkins
Anne T. Craig

200 N. Center Street
Northville, Michigan 48167-1416

*Telephone:* 810/349-6030
*Telefax:* 810/349-8982

Stephen J. Kirksey
Danielle McCluskey-Schink
Robert B. June

March 25, 1996

Mr. John Prosser, II, Vice President
Development, Acquisition and Public Relations
Health Partners, Inc.
17515 West Nine Mile Road
Suite 1185
Southfield, Michigan 48075

Re:   Michigan Jaycees - Prevention of Pediatric Traumatic Brain Injury

Dear John:

First of all, and as always, let me say that I hope this letter finds you and your family healthy, happy and enjoying the spring weather presently upon us. I have reviewed the materials that you sent me concerning the prevention of pediatric traumatic brain injury program that you are leading for the Michigan Jaycees, and I can tell you that I am absolutely astounded at the amount of work that you have done, and your devotion to this cause. On behalf of the Brain Injury Association, and maybe those children whose brain injuries will be prevented because of your efforts, I want to say thank you.

As a member of the board of directors of the Brain Injury Association, and the chairman of the development committee of the Brain Injury Association, I am most grateful for your efforts.

John, if there is anything that I can do to further assist you with this project, please do not hesitate to call upon me.

With regard to the golf outing on Friday, September 27, 1996 at 11:30 at the Pine Knob Golf Course, please know that I have marked this date down on my calendar. Please reserve a foursome for me at that time.

In closing, and as always, please accept my best wishes and prayers to you and your family for your good health, happiness and success in all of your endeavors.

As always, I remain,

Most respectfully yours,

CHARLES N. SIMKINS

**BRAIN INJURY ASSOCIATION, INC.**
(formerly National Head Injury Foundation, Inc.)

P.O. Box 218
Mt. Pleasant, NC 28124
(704) 436-6527 • FAX: (704) 436-9461

April 3, 1996

Mr. John Prosser II, Vice President
Development, Acquisition and Public Relations
Health Partners, Inc.
17515 West Nine Mile Road
Suite 1185
Southfield, Michigan 48075

Dear John:

I am happy to learn from Nick Simkins of your support for the Brain Injury Association and persons with traumatic brain injury. We especially appreciate your efforts toward the billboard campaign. Please know we are grateful for your help and if we can be of help to you in any way, let us know.

We appreciate Sharon Barefoot's introducing you to BIA's needed programs--and the Jaycees work in the area of prevention of pediatric traumatic brain injury. Thank you John, for all you do. Together we are making a difference!

Sincerely,

BRAIN INJURY ASSOCIATION, INC.

Martin B. Foil, Jr.
Chairman

jhs
cc - Mr. Nick Simkins

*The National Organization Serving People with Brain Injury • Promoting Prevention*

38

# Michigan Neuropsychological Society

26555 Evergreen Road, Suite #626
Southfield, MI 48076
(810) 350-9559

April 3, 1996

Mr. John G. Prosser II
17515 W. Nine Mile Road
Suite 1185
Southfield, MI  48075

> RE: Michigan Jaycees Pediatric Traumatic Brain Injury
> Prevention Campaign

Dear Mr. Prosser:

On behalf of the Michigan Neuropsychological Society, I would like to express our appreciation and endorsement of your campaign aimed toward prevention of head injuries in children.  I have been very impressed with your efforts and contributions in this respect thus far.  As you know, many pediatric head injuries arise out of sports activities.  Increased interest in skateboard and roller blading forms of recreation are creating additional challenges.  If all children wore helmets during these and other sports-related activities, we could tremendously reduce the lifelong suffering that many of these patients and families experience following central nervous system trauma.

Again, I commend you in your commitment to preventing traumatic brain injuries in this most vulnerable and young population.  Please let me know if there is anything else that I can do to support your cause.  Keep up the great work.

Very truly yours,

Dr. Bradley G. Sewick, President
Michigan Neuropsychological Society

*John Gwynne Prosser II*

STATE OF MICHIGAN

JOHN ENGLER, Governor

DEPARTMENT OF COMMUNITY HEALTH
JAMES K. HAVEMAN, JR., Director

**COMMUNITY PUBLIC HEALTH AGENCY**

3423 N. MARTIN L. KING JR. BLVD.
PO BOX 30195
LANSING, MI 48909

April 8, 1996

John G. Prosser II
Michigan Jaycees State Chairman
17515 West Nine Mile Road
Suite 1185
Southfield, MI 48075

Dear Mr. Prosser:

I am writing in support of the pediatric traumatic brain injury prevention efforts of the Michigan Jaycees. As you know, injuries to the brain stand out as the most catastrophic in terms of their numbers, severity, human suffering and economic loss, and associated health care, rehabilitation and related costs. Injuries are now being recognized as a serious public health problem and many, if not most, are preventable.

Bicycle helmets have been strongly recommended as a way to prevent and reduce the severity of brain injuries as a result of bicycle crashes. A study of the effectiveness of bicycle helmets demonstrated that there was an 88% reduction in the risk of brain injury in a crash when a bicycle helmet was used. Thus, increasing the prevalence of helmet use among young people is a vital step in reducing the risk of serious and fatal brain injuries resulting from bicycle crashes.

Over the past five years, the Unintentional Injury Section has been involved in promoting the use of helmets by developing and disseminating educational materials and community-based prevention programs for children. If you would like more information on our helmet materials, please contact Heather Festerling at (517) 335-9519.

I commend the Michigan Jaycees for undertaking the important task of educating the public on the importance of helmet use and applaud your efforts to protect Michigan's children.

Sincerely,

Linda Harner, Chief
Unintentional Injury Section

**THE DETROIT LIONS, INC.** 1200 FEATHERSTONE RD. / PONTIAC, MICHIGAN 48342 / GENERAL OFFICE (810) 335-4131
TICKET OFFICE: (810) 335-4151

April 23, 1996

Mr. John G. Prosser II
Vice President/Development,
Acquisition & Public Relations
c/o Health Partners Inc.
17515 West Nine Mile Road
Suite 1185
Southfield, MI 48075

Dear Mr. Prosser:

On behalf of the Detroit Lions, I commend you and the Michigan Jaycees on your efforts in support of the Brain Injury Association. In particular, I salute you for focusing your activities on the prevention of pediatric traumatic brain injury.

It is shocking the number of youngsters and young adults who die or suffer from disabilities as the result of a head trauma each year. The vast majority of these injuries could be avoided by wearing something we in football take so much for granted --- a helmet. Barry Sanders or Herman Moore would never go on the field without wearing his helmet, nor should a child go biking, roller blading, etc. without his or her helmet. It seems so simple, so obvious, yet so often forgotten, avoided or ignored.

Best wishes, Jaycees, on success. You have a difficult challenge before you --- but when you win, we all win.

The Lions are cheering for you!

Sincerely,

Tim Pendell
Director of Community Relations and
Detroit Lions Charities

41

**BRAIN INJURY ASSOCIATION, INC.**
(formerly National Head Injury Foundation, Inc.)

1776 Massachusetts Avenue, N.W.
Suite 100
Washington, DC 20036-1904
(202) 296-6443 • Fax: (202) 296-8850

April 26, 1996

Mr. John Prosser II
Vice President
Development, Acquisition and Public Relations
Health Partners, Inc.
17515 West Nine Mile Road, Suite 1185
Southfield, MI   48075

Dear Mr. Prosser:

Please accept our profound gratitude for your efforts on behalf of prevention of traumatic brain injury. At the Brain Injury Association, Inc. and our collaborating center, the Violence and Brain Injury Institute, we are grateful for the success you have had in bringing greater awareness and understanding to your community and state about the need to address the epidemic of TBI. We are proud of your support.

The Brain Injury Association of Michigan is acknowledged to have one of the best bicycle safety programs in the country and our national prevention program, the Be HeadSmart® Community Project, is growing at a rapid pace. With assistance from committed people like you, we are seeing results. Please contact Mr. Will Hatcher at (703) 299-0699 for more information about our programs or to discuss how we might be of assistance to you.

Again, congratulations to you for your outstanding contribution toward our mutual goal of eradicating traumatic brain injury!

Sincerely,

*George A. Zitnay, Ph.D.*

George A. Zitnay, PhD
President and CEO

*The National Organization Serving People with Brain Injury • Promoting Prevention*

42

# MICHIGAN JAYCEES

Domino's Pizza and the Michigan Jaycees proudly present; A Campaign, For the Prevention of Pediatric Traumatic Brain Injury. The Leading Killer and cause of disability in children and young adults.

FACTS Most TBI injuries could be prevented if children of all ages wore a helmet while enjoying activities which have the potential for Head Trauma, such as Roller Skating or Blading, Bike Riding, Skate Boarding, Trampolines, etc....

WE HAVE 3 GOALS AND WE NEED YOUR HELP!

#1. Educate Parents & Children regarding the facts surrounding TBI, and that they must wear a Helmet, (your example as an adult role model is most significant)

#2. To raise money for our Billboard Campaign (Gannett Outdoor has donated 3000 spaces). We are raising money for the printing of them. Sample Billboard: *"KID'S YOUR SKULL ISN'T AS THICK AS YOUR PARENTS THINK – WEAR A HELMET"*

#3. To recruit Miciganders to join the Jaycees and become community activists on this very important issue! *PLEASE TAKE ACTION TODAY.* Our Children are our most precious asset. Please call the Michigan Jaycees State Headquarters at (517) 487-6077, you will be referred to your local chapter President. We desire to find block captains statewide who will distribute bright colored TBI Fact Sheets to their neighbors. JUST TELL US HOW MANY YOU WANT! All fact sheet printing and mailing provided courtesy of Great lakes Rehabilitation Hospital in Southfield, Michigan.

FACTS: 2 Million TBI per year in USA, 500,000 require hospitalization, 75,000 to 100,000 Americans die every year from TBI, of those who survive 70,000-90,000 will endure lifelong depilitathy loss of function, 2000 will exist in vegetative state, more deaths in past 12 years in USA than All American Battle Deaths of all wars from found of the Republic. A survivor typically faces intensive medical costs in excess of 4 million dollars, Research into control & prevention receives less than one penny of every Federal spent on Medical Research. Brain injuries account for 43% of deaths to young school aged children far surpassing any other cause.

STATE CHAIRMAN
MICHIGAN JAYCEES

_____ \* \* \* \* \* \* \* \*

Fax (810) 423-3485

Southfield, Michigan 48075
17515 West Nine Mile Rd.
Suite 1185
(810) 423-3466
1 (800) 969-7723
In Michigan

**JOHN G. PROSSER II**
Vice President
Development, Acquisition
& Public Relations

THE UNITED STATES JAYCEES
PUBLIC SERVICE ANNOUNCEMENT

PEDIATRIC BRAIN INJURY PREVENTION CAMPAIGN

THE HONORABLE GEORGE BUSH
SPOKESPERSON

one minute script

Hello, I am President George Bush, with a message for you!

Presently BRAIN INJURY in America is the leading cause of death and disability to our children and grandchildren! I am working with the UNITED STATES JAYCEES (Junior Chamber of Commerce) to encourage you to help us by VOLUNTEERING your time and energy, and promoting Pediatric Brain Injury Prevention---------Please encourage everyone you know, Parents and Children, to wear a Safety Helmet during any sporting activity!

CHILDREN please remember: **"Your skull is'nt as thick as your parents think—so be good and wear your helmet!"**

Will you please join us in this community service effort to protect our greatest natural resource, our children?

Join me and get involved with one of America's great leadership organizations, the United States Jaycees. For your free Brain Injury fact sheets to give to your neighbors, and a referral to your local Jaycee Chapter president, please call (918) 584-2481 or write to U.S. Jaycees at P.O.Box 7, Tulsa, Oaklahoma 74102.

Your committment will make the difference!

THANK YOU

*phone number will run on screen throughout announcement*

John G. Prosser II, Chairman, Pediatric Brain Injury Prevention Campaign
541 West Iroquois, Pontiac, Michigan 48341     office   (810) 423-3466
                                              fax     (810) 423 -3465
                                              or      (810) 335 -0999
JCI Senator #48006
Pontiac Jaycee
Michigan Jaycee
U.S. Jaycee

**BRAIN INJURY ASSOCIATION, INC.**
(formerly National Head Injury Foundation, Inc.)

1776 Massachusetts Avenue, N.W.
Suite 100
Washington, DC 20036-1904
(202) 296-6443 • Fax: (202) 296-8850

**FOR IMMEDIATE RELEASE**

CONTACT: Tamela Reid
202/296-6443
John G. Prosser, II
810/423-3466

## MICHIGAN JAYCEES AND DOMINO'S PIZZA SPONSOR SUMMER CAMPAIGN FOCUSING ON BRAIN INJURY PREVENTION

(WASHINGTON, DC, June 24, 1996) - The Brain Injury Association (BIA) is pleased to announce that the Michigan Jaycees and Domino's Pizza are sponsoring a summer campaign on pediatric brain injury prevention. Fliers containing brain safety tips are to be distributed in southeastern Michigan by Domino's Pizza stores through September 2, 1996. Children can bring the flier and their bike helmet into participating Domino's stores and receive a free order of breadsticks. The campaign will also include a golf tournament to be held September 27, 1996 at the Pine Knob Golf Course in Clarkston. This golf tournament is coordinated through Health Partners and the Pontiac Jaycees. Proceeds from the golf tournament will go to BIA's "Wear a Helmet" billboard campaign.

Summer is the time of year when most Americans relax, kickback and enjoy the outdoors. For many people, this summer will mark a change in their lives forever. These people will sustain a brain injury. Brain injury is an insult to the brain, not of degenerative or congenital nature but caused by an external physical force that may produce a diminished or altered state of consciousness, which results in an impairment of cognitive abilities or physical functioning. The cost of brain injury in the US is estimated to be $48.3 billion annually, most of this expense is

-more-

*The National Organization Serving People with Brain Injury • Promoting Prevention*

paid for by the taxpayer through Medicare and Medicaid. Individual costs average $4 million a lifetime.

**EVERY 15 SECONDS A PERSON RECEIVES A BRAIN INJURY. Brain injury is the leading cause of death for Americans under 45 years of age.** It is estimated that brain injury claims more than 56,000 American lives annually and about 373,000 people are hospitalized each year as a result of brain injury. Of these, 99,000 individuals sustain moderate to severe brain injuries resulting in lifelong disabling conditions.

**BRAIN INJURY IS PREVENTABLE.** Vehicle crashes are the leading cause of brain injury. Other major causes include falls, firearms, sports and recreation. Brain injuries account for 62% of bicycle-related deaths, for 33% of bicycle-related emergency department visits and for 67% of bicycle-related hospital admissions. Wearing a helmet while biking, in-line skating, or skateboarding reduces the incidence of brain injury by 74-85%.

The Brain Injury Association believes in promoting awareness, understanding and prevention. BIA currently manages several prevention campaigns. One such campaign is the HeadSmart™ School Program which provides elementary and preschool educators with the tools to teach youngsters about the brain as well as brain injury and violence prevention. BIA also offers a toll-free Family HelpLine (1-800-444-6443) for individuals to speak with trained information and resource specialists who can assist with questions about brain injury.

For more information on brain injury, HeadSmart™, and other activities of the Brain Injury Association, contact Tamela Reid, Public Relations Manager at 202/296-6443.

## THE COST OF PREVENTING INJURIES AT ALL COSTS

The 20-year-old plumber had climbed to the roof of the house being built near Dayton, Ohio, to size up the job ahead of him. He didn't know that roofers had placed a sheet of styrofoam over the hole left for the chimney, then covered it with a piece of plywood. When the plumber stepped on the spot, the unsteady coverings gave way. He plunged three floors to the basement, landing on his head.

"You tell me. Could we have prevented this?" asks Mary McCarthy, a doctor who heads the trauma program at Dayton's Miami Valley Hospital and a nascent effort to combat injuries in surrounding Montgomery County. "If we're losing 20-year-old kids in construction accidents, shouldn't we be trying? We're not here just to pick up the pieces and to give lectures about safety. We need to be intervening and evaluating sites for safety."

McCarthy and her trauma surgeon comrades like to use the slogan "Trauma is no accident." In fact, McCarthy calls trauma a disease that needs to be tracked and attacked like tuberculosis and other plagues on the public. Thomas Breitenbach, the CEO of Miami Valley, agrees with her—and so do the chief executives at five other hospitals in the area. Through the Dayton Area Hospital Association, they formed and funded the Injury Prevention Center of Greater Dayton. They've recruited additional partners for their venture, including the school of medicine and other departments at Wright State University, a community college, and a major HMO, United HealthCare of Ohio.

McCarthy cites the construction accident as a likely future direction for the center, which emphasizes education, intervention and aggressive follow-up research. For starters, the center combed through emergency department reports and other statistics and came up with four areas needing attention: bicycle injuries, gun violence and safety, falls among the elderly, and car accidents involving teen drivers.

With the center barely a year old, most of these projects are just getting off the ground. "I'm very frustrated when I take care of injuries that could have been prevented by simple things, like keeping a gun locked up or wearing a bicycle helmet," says McCarthy. "In the aftermath, I see whole lives destroyed, not to mention the costs to their families and our society. But I didn't have a way to address it until now."

McCarthy got her chance two years ago, when Breit-enbach asked his senior managers for proposals focusing on unmet needs in the community, especially those aimed at preventable problems. Breitenbach says he was inspired by his work as chairman-elect of a local council of business executives overseeing a $70 million property tax levy that was set up to fund the county health department and to fight abuse on several fronts—children, alcohol and drugs.

He and his board liked McCarthy's idea for an injury prevention center because it touched on all those areas and

### DAYTON, OHIO

▶ **THE PROBLEM:** Injuries kill more than 500 people each year in Dayton and surrounding Montgomery County, while more than 6,000 injured require hospital care. Emergency departments rack up more than 150,000 visits caused by injuries. The county's rate of 34.9 injury-related deaths per 100,000 people well exceeds the 29.3 target set by Healthy People 2000.

▶ **THE PLAYERS:** Prompted by Miami Valley Hospital (which runs the area's largest trauma center), six members of the Greater Dayton Hospital Association joined in creating the Injury Prevention Center. Other partners include business owners, Wright State University, United HealthCare of Ohio, and Sinclair Community College.

▶ **THE PLAN:** Unify emergency department coding and sift through current reports to target four problem areas: Car crashes involving teens and alcohol, gun violence and safety, falls among the elderly, and bicycle safety.

▶ **THE RESULTS:** Though just getting started, partners used an early grant to buy infant car seats and bicycle helmets for the poor. A bike shop provides safe, rebuilt bikes. Other steps: starting an exercise program and home safety inspection for the elderly; widening an existing Drive Smart program run by emergency nurses and targeted at teens; and working with schools to warn children about the danger of guns.

could draw many existing, smaller programs under one umbrella. So, at his board's urging, he took the idea to the hospital association and won the support of his colleagues.

*Dayton's Injury Prevention Center not only fits young cyclists with helmets, but monitors parks and other sites to see whether they actually wear them.*

Several area hospitals already had launched bike or home safety, but the center's pooled resources should expand their reach and effectiveness. "The whole community comes out ahead," Breitenbach says. He plans to expand the center's programs to an 11-county area surrounding Dayton.

Though preventing injuries should logically lead to a healthier community and position everyone for growth in prepaid health plans, Breitenbach concedes that lining up the $500,000 to $600,000 needed to operate the program each year isn't always an easy sell. An employer may balk at spending money on prevention because the benefits of healthier workers may be years in coming, when they work for someone else. "The costs and benefits accrue to different people," Breitenbach says. "The benefits are long term, but the costs are immediate." ∎

# Website for Michigan Automobile insurance laws and related subjects

www.legislature.mi.gov

then go to Laws, then go to frequent requests, then insurance, and then No Fault you can choose PDF format or HTML. Here you will find an outline of the complete no fault law by section with full descriptions and full chapters. It is in the back of this book also!

www.legislature.mi.gov

here you will also find a complete Plan of Operation of the Michigan Catastrophic Claim Association which since its inception in 1978 has processed 18,000 claims over that period of 27 years.

## Resource Websites

www.ahcpr.gov    Agency for Health Care Research and Quality

www.aapainmanagement.org    American Academy of pain management

www.theacpa.org    American Chronic Pain association

www.paincare.org    National Foundation for the treatment of pain

www.ama-assn.org    American Medical association

www.aapmr.org    American Academy of Physical Medicine and Rehabilitation

www.rehabnurse.org    Association of Rehabilitation Nurses

www.CMSA.org    Case Management Society of America

www.biausa.org    The Brain Injury Association of America

# Michigan No Fault Law Outline

| Document | Type | Description |
|---|---|---|
| Section 500.3101 | Section | Security for payment of benefits required; period security required to be in effect; deletion of coverage; definitions; policy of insurance or other method of providing security; filing proof of security; "insurer" defined. |
| Section 500.3101a | Section | Providing certificates of insurance to policyholder; filing copy with secretary of state; vehicle identification number as proof of vehicle insurance; prohibited acts; misdemeanor; penalty. |
| Section 500.3101b | Section | Providing proof of vehicle insurance pursuant to 500.3101a(2). |
| Section 500.3101c | Section | Standard certified statement. |
| Section 500.3102 | Section | Nonresident owner or registrant of motor vehicle or motorcycle to maintain security for payment of benefits; operation of motor vehicle or motorcycle by owner, registrant, or other person without security; penalty; failure to produce evidence of security; rebuttable presumption. |
| Section 500.3103 | Section | Owner or registrant of motorcycle; security required; offering security for payment of first-party medical benefits; rates, deductibles, and provisions. |
| Section 500.3104 | Section | Catastrophic claims association. |
| Section 500.3105 | Section | Insurer liable for personal protection benefits without regard to fault; "bodily injury" and "accidental bodily injury" defined. |

Section 500.3106　Section　Accidental bodily injury arising out of ownership, operation, maintenance, or use of parked vehicle as motor vehicle; conditions.

Section 500.3107　Section　Expenses and work loss for which personal protection benefits payable.

Section 500.3107a　Section　Basis of work loss for certain injured persons.

Section 500.3107b　Section　Reimbursement or coverage for certain expenses not required; conditional effective date of subdivision (b).

Section 500.3108　Section　Survivor's loss; benefits.

Section 500.3109　Section　Subtraction of other benefits from personal protection benefits; "injured person" defined; deductible provision.

Section 500.3109a　Section　Offering deductibles and exclusions reasonably related to other health and accident coverage; rates; approval; applicability.

Section 500.3110　Section　Dependents of deceased person; termination of dependency; accrual of personal protection benefits.

Section 500.3111　Section　Payment of personal protection benefits for accident occurring out of state.

Section 500.3112　Section　Persons to whom personal protection benefits payable; discharge of insurer's liability.

Section 500.3113　Section　Persons not entitled to personal protection benefits.

| Section 500.3143 | Section | Assignment of right to future benefits void. |
| Section 500.3145 | Section | Limitation of actions for recovery of personal or property protection benefits; notice of injury. |
| Section 500.3146 | Section | Limitation of action by insurer for recovery or indemnity. |
| Section 500.3148 | Section | Attorney's fee. |
| Section 500.3151 | Section | Submission to mental or physical examination. |
| Section 500.3152 | Section | Report of mental or physical examination. |
| Section 500.3153 | Section | Court orders as to noncompliance with 500.3151 and 500.3152. |
| Section 500.3157 | Section | Charges for products, services, and accommodations where treatment rendered. |
| Section 500.3158 | Section | Statement of earnings; report and records from medical institution. |
| Section 500.3159 | Section | Discovery. |
| Section 500.3163 | Section | Certification by admitted and non-admitted insurers as to protection of out-of-state resident; rights and immunities of insurer and insured; benefits to out-of-state resident; limitation. |
| Section 500.3171 | Section | Assigned claims facility and plan; organization and maintenance; participation; costs; rules. |

55

| | |
|---|---|
| Section 500.3172 | Section | Conditions to obtaining personal protection insurance benefits through assigned claims plan; collection of unpaid benefits; reimbursement from defaulting insurers; reduction of benefits; applicability of subsection (2); definitions; effect of dispute between insurers. |
| Section 500.3173 | Section | Certain persons disqualified from receiving benefits under assigned claims plans. |
| Section 500.3173a | Section | Eligibility for benefits; initial determination; denial; notice. |
| Section 500.3174 | Section | Notice of claim through assigned claims plan; assignment of claim; notice to claimant; commencement of action by claimant. |
| Section 500.3175 | Section | Rules for assignment of claims; duties of insurer to whom claims assigned; compromises and settlements; rules; limitation on action to enforce rights; interest on delinquent payments; installment payments. |
| Section 500.3176 | Section | Taking costs into account in making and regulating rates. |
| Section 500.3177 | Section | Recovery by insurer of benefits and costs from owner or registrant of uninsured motor vehicle; written agreement to pay judgment in installments; notice. |
| Section 500.3179 | Section | Act applicable October 1, 1973. |

The Michigan Legislature Website is a free service of the Legislative Internet Technology Team in cooperation with the Michigan Legislative Council, the Michigan House of Representatives, and the Michigan Senate.

The information obtained from this site is not intended to replace official versions of that information and is subject to revision. The Legislature presents this information, without warranties, express or implied, regarding the information's accuracy, timeliness, or completeness. If you believe the information is inaccurate, out-of-date, or incomplete or if you have problems accessing or reading the information, please send your concerns to the appropriate agency using the online Comment Form.

Please call the Michigan Law Library at (517) 373-0630 for legal reference questions.

# Complete Michigan

# No Fault Law

# THE INSURANCE CODE OF 1956 (EXCERPT)

## Act 218 of 1956

**500.3101 Security for payment of benefits required; period security required to be in effect; deletion of coverage; definitions; policy of insurance or other method of providing security; filing proof of security; insured defined.**

Sec. 3101.

(1) The owner or registrant of a motor vehicle required to be registered in this state shall maintain security for payment of benefits under personal protection insurance, property protection insurance, and residual liability insurance. Security shall only be required to be in effect during the period the motor vehicle is driven or moved upon a highway. Notwithstanding any other provision in this act, an insurer that has issued an automobile insurance policy on a motor vehicle that is not driven or moved upon a highway may allow the insured owner or registrant of the motor vehicle to delete a portion of the coverages under the policy and maintain the comprehensive coverage portion of the policy in effect.

(2) As used in this chapter:

(a)Automobile insurance means that term as defined in section 2102.

(b) Highway means that term as defined in section 20 of the Michigan vehicle code, Act No. 300 of the Public

Acts of 1949, being section 257.20 of the Michigan Compiled Laws.

(c) Motorcycle means a vehicle having a saddle or seat for the use of the rider, designed to travel on not more than 3 wheels in contact with the ground, which is equipped with a motor that exceeds 50 cubic centimeters piston displacement. The wheels on any attachment to the vehicle shall not be considered as wheels in contact with the ground. Motorcycle does not include a moped, as defined in section 32b of the Michigan vehicle code, Act No. 300 of the Public Acts of 1949, being section 257.32b of the Michigan Compiled Laws.

(d) Motorcycle accident means a loss involving the ownership, operation, maintenance, or use of a motorcycle as a motorcycle, but not involving the ownership, operation, maintenance, or use of a motor vehicle as a motor vehicle.

(e) Motor vehicle means a vehicle, including a trailer, operated or designed for operation upon a public highway by power other than muscular power which has more than 2 wheels. Motor vehicle does not include a motorcycle or a moped, as defined in section 32b of Act No. 300 of the Public Acts of 1949, being section 257.32b of the Michigan Compiled Laws. Motor vehicle does not include a farm tractor or other implement of husbandry which is not subject to the registration requirements of the Michigan vehicle code pursuant to section 216 of the Michigan vehicle code, Act No. 300 of the Public Acts of 1949, being section 257.216 of the Michigan Compiled Laws.

(f) Motor vehicle accident means a loss involving the ownership, operation, maintenance, or use of a motor vehicle as a motor vehicle regardless of whether the accident also involves the ownership, operation, maintenance, or use of a motorcycle as a motorcycle.

(g) Owner means any of the following:

(i) A person renting a motor vehicle or having the use thereof, under a lease or otherwise, for a period that is greater than 30 days.

(ii) A person who holds the legal title to a vehicle, other than a person engaged in the business of leasing motor vehicles who is the lessor of a motor vehicle pursuant to a lease providing for the use of the motor vehicle by the lessee for a period that is greater than 30 days.

(iii) A person who has the immediate right of possession of a motor vehicle under an installment sale contract.

(h) Registrant does not include a person engaged in the business of leasing motor vehicles who is the lessor of a motor vehicle pursuant to a lease providing for the use of the motor vehicle by the lessee for a period that is greater than 30 days.

(3) Security may be provided under a policy issued by an insurer duly authorized to transact business in this state which affords insurance for the payment of benefits described in subsection (1). A policy of insurance represented or sold as providing security shall be deemed to provide insurance for the payment of the benefits.

(4) Security required by subsection (1) may be provided by any other method approved by the secretary of state as affording security equivalent to that afforded by a policy of insurance, if proof of the security is filed and continuously maintained with the secretary of state throughout the period the motor vehicle is driven or moved upon a highway. The person filing the security has all the obligations and rights of an insurer under this chapter. When the context permits, insurer as used in this chapter, includes any person filing the security as provided in this section.

**History:** Add. 1972, Act 294, Eff. Mar. 30, 1973 ;-- Am. 1975, Act 329, Eff. Mar. 31, 1976 ;-- Am. 1977, Act 54, Imd. Eff. July 6, 1977 ;-- Am. 1980, Act 445, Imd. Eff. Jan. 15, 1981 ;-- Am. 1984, Act 84, Imd. Eff. Apr. 19, 1984 ;-- Am. 1987, Act 168, Imd. Eff. Nov. 9, 1987 ;-- Am. 1988, Act 126, Imd. Eff. May 23, 1988

**Constitutionality:** Subsection (1) of this section is unconstitutional but subsection (2) does not violate the due process and equal protection clauses. Shavers v. Attorney General, 402 Mich. 554, 267 N.W.2d 72 (1978).

**Compiler's Notes:** Act 143 of 1993, which amended this section, was submitted to the people by referendum petition (as Proposal C) and rejected by a majority of the votes cast at the November 8, 1994, general election.

**Popular Name:** Act 218

**Popular Name:** Essential Insurance

**Popular Name:** No-Fault Insurance

© 2004 Legislative Council, State of Michigan

# THE INSURANCE CODE OF 1956 (EXCERPT)

## Act 218 of 1956

**500.3101a Providing certificates of insurance to policyholder; filing copy with secretary of state; vehicle identification number as proof of vehicle insurance; prohibited acts; misdemeanor; penalty.**

Sec. 3101a.

(1) An insurer, in conjunction with the issuance of an automobile insurance policy, as defined in section 3303, shall provide 2 certificates of insurance for each insured vehicle. The insurer shall mark 1 of the certificates as the secretary of state's copy, which copy, except as otherwise provided in subsection (2), shall be filed with the secretary of state by the policyholder upon application for a vehicle registration. The secretary of state shall not maintain the certificate of insurance received under this subsection on file.

(2) The secretary of state shall accept as proof of vehicle insurance a transmission, in the format required by the secretary of state, of the insured vehicle's vehicle identification number. Vehicle identification numbers received by the secretary of state under this subsection are confidential and shall not be disclosed to any person except pursuant to an order by a court of competent jurisdiction in connection with a claim or fraud investigation or prosecution. The transmission to the secretary of state of a vehicle identification number is proof of insurance to the secretary of state for motor

vehicle registration purposes only and is not evidence that a policy of insurance actually exists between an insurer and an individual.

(3) A person who supplies false information to the secretary of state under this section or who issues or uses an altered, fraudulent, or counterfeit certificate of insurance is guilty of a misdemeanor punishable by imprisonment for not more than 1 year, or a fine of not more than $1,000.00, or both.

**History:** Add. 1980, Act 461, Eff. Apr. 1, 1981 ;-- Am. 1995, Act 288, Imd. Eff. Jan. 9, 1996 ;-- Am. 1996, Act 456, Imd. Eff. Dec. 23, 1996

**Compiler's Notes:** Act 143 of 1993, which amended this section, was submitted to the people by referendum petition (as Proposal C) and rejected by a majority of the votes cast at the November 8, 1994, general election.

**Popular Name:** Act 218

**Popular Name:** Essential Insurance

**Popular Name:** No-Fault Insurance

Â© 2004 Legislative Council, State of Michigan

# THE INSURANCE CODE OF 1956 (EXCERPT)

## Act 218 of 1956

## 500.3101b Providing proof of vehicle insurance pursuant to 500.3101a(2).

Sec. 3101b.

All insurers who choose to provide proof of vehicle insurance to the secretary of state pursuant to section 3101a (2) shall do so through the insurance verification board created in section 227b of the Michigan vehicle code, Act No. 300 of the Public Acts of 1949, being section 257.227b of the Michigan Compiled Laws, or the organization selected by the board. If that board or the organization selected by the board is not operational and able to transmit to the secretary of state by June 1, 1996 or if the board or organization stops transmitting proof of vehicle insurance by vehicle identification number to the secretary of state, an insurer who chooses to provide proof of vehicle insurance to the secretary of state pursuant to section 3101a (2) may do so directly and is not required to do so through the board or organization. Choosing to provide proof of vehicle insurance pursuant to section 227b of the Michigan vehicle code, Act No. 300 of the Public Acts of 1949, being section 257.227b of the Michigan Compiled Laws is not a state mandate and may not be identified on the automobile insurance declarations page as a state mandate or a state mandated assessment. Automobile insurers in this state shall not charge their policyholders more than a sufficient amount to cover the cost of any assessment for this program.

**History:** Add. 1995, Act 288, Imd. Eff. Jan. 9, 1996

**Popular Name:** Act 218

**Popular Name:** Essential Insurance

**Popular Name:** No-Fault Insurance

Â© 2004 Legislative Council, State of Michigan

# THE INSURANCE CODE OF 1956 (EXCERPT)
## Act 218 of 1956

## 500.3101c Standard certified statement.

Sec. 3101c.

The commissioner shall prescribe a standard certified statement that automobile insurers shall use to show pursuant to section 227a(1)(a) of the Michigan vehicle code, Act No. 300 of the Public Acts of 1949, being section 257.227a of the Michigan Compiled Laws, that a vehicle is insured under a 6-month prepaid, non-cancelable policy.

**History:** Add. 1995, Act 288, Imd. Eff. Jan. 9, 1996

**Popular Name:** Act 218

**Popular Name:** Essential Insurance

**Popular Name:** No-Fault Insurance

Â© 2004 Legislative Council, State of Michigan

## THE INSURANCE CODE OF 1956 (EXCERPT)

### Act 218 of 1956

**500.3102 Nonresident owner or registrant of motor vehicle or motorcycle to maintain security for payment of benefits; operation of motor vehicle or motorcycle by owner, registrant, or other person without security; penalty; failure to produce evidence of security; rebuttable presumption.**

Sec. 3102.

(1) A nonresident owner or registrant of a motor vehicle or motorcycle not registered in this state shall not operate or permit the motor vehicle or motorcycle to be operated in this state for an aggregate of more than 30 days in any calendar year unless he or she continuously maintains security for the payment of benefits pursuant to this chapter.

(2) An owner or registrant of a motor vehicle or motorcycle with respect to which security is required, who operates the motor vehicle or motorcycle or permits it to be operated upon a public highway in this state, without having in full force and effect security complying with this section or section 3101 or 3103 is guilty of a misdemeanor. A person who operates a motor vehicle or motorcycle upon a public highway in this state with the knowledge that the owner or registrant does not have security in full force and effect is guilty of a misdemeanor. A person convicted of a misdemeanor under this section shall be fined not less

than $200.00 nor more than $500.00, imprisoned for not more than 1 year, or both.

(3) The failure of a person to produce evidence that a motor vehicle or motorcycle has in full force and effect security complying with this section or section 3101 or 3103 on the date of the issuance of the citation, creates a rebuttable presumption in a prosecution under subsection (2) that the motor vehicle or motorcycle did not have in full force and effect security complying with this section or section 3101 or 3103 on the date of the issuance of the citation.

**History:** Add. 1972, Act 294, Eff. Mar. 30, 1973 ;-- Am. 1975, Act 329, Eff. Mar. 31, 1976 ;-- Am. 1979, Act 145, Imd. Eff. Nov. 13, 1979 ;-- Am. 1980, Act 446, Imd. Eff. Jan. 15, 1981 ;-- Am. 1987, Act 187, Eff. Mar. 30, 1988 ;-- Am. 1990, Act 79, Imd. Eff. May 24, 1990

**Popular Name:** Act 218

**Popular Name:** Essential Insurance

**Popular Name:** No-Fault Insurance

Â© 2004 Legislative Council, State of Michigan

## THE INSURANCE CODE OF 1956 (EXCERPT)

### Act 218 of 1956

**500.3103 Owner or registrant of motorcycle; security required; offering security for payment of first-party medical benefits; rates, deductibles, and provisions.**

Sec. 3103.

(1) An owner or registrant of a motorcycle shall provide security against loss resulting from liability imposed by law for property damage, bodily injury, or death suffered by a person arising out of the ownership, maintenance, or use of that motorcycle. The security shall conform with the requirements of section 3009(1).

(2) Each insurer transacting insurance in this state which affords coverage for a motorcycle as described in subsection (1) also shall offer, to an owner or registrant of a motorcycle, security for the payment of first-party medical benefits only, in increments of $5,000.00, payable in the event the owner or registrant is involved in a motorcycle accident. An insurer providing first-party medical benefits may offer, at appropriate premium rates, deductibles, provisions for the coordination of these benefits, and provisions for the subtraction of other benefits provided or required to be provided under the laws of any state or the federal government, subject to the prior approval of the commissioner. These deductibles and provisions shall apply only to benefits payable to the person named in

the policy, the spouse of the insured, and any relative of either domiciled in the same household.

**History:** Add. 1975, Act 329, Eff. Mar. 31, 1976 ;-- Am. 1977, Act 54, Imd. Eff. July 6, 1977 ;-- Am. 1980, Act 445, Eff. Jan. 15, 1981 ;-- Am. 1986, Act 173, Imd. Eff. July 7, 1986

**Constitutionality:** The legislative scheme which allows motorcyclists to receive no-fault benefits for personal injuries without requiring them to maintain no-fault security does not deny automobile drivers equal protection or due process of law. Underhill v. Safeco Insurance Company, 407 Mich. 175, 284 N.W.2d 463 (1979).

**Popular Name:** Act 218

**Popular Name:** Essential Insurance

**Popular Name:** No-Fault Insurance

# THE INSURANCE CODE OF 1956 (EXCERPT)

## Act 218 of 1956

### 500.3104 Catastrophic claims association.

Sec. 3104.

(1) An unincorporated, nonprofit association to be known as the catastrophic claims association, hereinafter referred to as the association, is created. Each insurer engaged in writing insurance coverage that provide the security required by section 3101(1) within this state, as a condition of its authority to transact insurance in this state, shall be a member of the association and shall be bound by the plan of operation of the association. Each insurer engaged in writing insurance coverage that provide the security required by section 3103(1) within this state, as a condition of its authority to transact insurance in this state, shall be considered a member of the association, but only for purposes of premiums under subsection (7)(d). Except as expressly provided in this section, the association is not subject to any laws of this state with respect to insurers, but in all other respects the association is subject to the laws of this state to the extent that the association would be if it were an insurer organized and subsisting under chapter 50.

(2) The association shall provide and each member shall accept indemnification for 100% of the amount of ultimate loss sustained under personal protection

insurance coverage in excess of the following amounts in each loss occurrence:

(a) For a motor vehicle accident policy issued or renewed before July 1, 2002, $250,000.00.

(b) For a motor vehicle accident policy issued or renewed during the period July 1, 2002 to June 30, 2003, $300,000.00.

(c) For a motor vehicle accident policy issued or renewed during the period July 1, 2003 to June 30, 2004, $325,000.00.

(d) For a motor vehicle accident policy issued or renewed during the period July 1, 2004 to June 30, 2005, $350,000.00.

(e) For a motor vehicle accident policy issued or renewed during the period July 1, 2005 to June 30, 2006, $375,000.00.

(f) For a motor vehicle accident policy issued or renewed during the period July 1, 2006 to June 30, 2007, $400,000.00.

(g) For a motor vehicle accident policy issued or renewed during the period July 1, 2007 to June 30, 2008, $420,000.00.

(h) For a motor vehicle accident policy issued or renewed during the period July 1, 2008 to June 30, 2009, $440,000.00.

(i) For a motor vehicle accident policy issued or renewed during the period July 1, 2009 to June 30, 2010, $460,000.00.

(j) For a motor vehicle accident policy issued or renewed during the period July 1, 2010 to June 30, 2011, $480,000.00.

(k) For a motor vehicle accident policy issued or renewed during the period July 1, 2011 to June 30, 2013, $500,000.00. Beginning July 1, 2013, this $500,000.00 amount shall be increased biennially on July 1 of each odd-numbered year, for policies issued or renewed before July 1 of the following odd-numbered year, by the lesser of 6% or the consumer price index, and rounded to the nearest $5,000.00. This biennial adjustment shall be calculated by the association by January 1 of the year of its July 1 effective date.

(3) An insurer may withdraw from the association only upon ceasing to write insurance that provides the security required by section 3101(1) in this state.

(4) An insurer whose membership in the association has been terminated by withdrawal shall continue to be bound by the plan of operation, and upon withdrawal, all unpaid premiums that have been charged to the withdrawing member are payable as of the effective date of the withdrawal.

(5) An unsatisfied net liability to the association of an insolvent member shall be assumed by and apportioned among the remaining members of the association as provided in the plan of operation. The association has

all rights allowed by law on behalf of the remaining members against the estate or funds of the insolvent member for sums due the association.

(6) If a member has been merged or consolidated into another insurer or another insurer has reinsured a member's entire business that provides the security required by section 3101(1) in this state, the member and successors in interest of the member remain liable for the member's obligations.

(7) The association shall do all of the following on behalf of the members of the association:

(a) Assume 100% of all liability as provided in subsection (2).

(b) Establish procedures by which members shall promptly report to the association each claim that, on the basis of the injuries or damages sustained, may reasonably be anticipated to involve the association if the member is ultimately held legally liable for the injuries or damages. Solely for the purpose of reporting claims, the member shall in all instances consider itself legally liable for the injuries or damages. The member shall also advise the association of subsequent developments likely to materially affect the interest of the association in the claim.

(c) Maintain relevant loss and expense data relative to all liabilities of the association and require each member to furnish statistics, in connection with liabilities of the association, at the times and in the form and detail as may be required by the plan of operation.

(d) In a manner provided for in the plan of operation, calculate and charge to members of the association a total premium sufficient to cover the expected losses and expenses of the association that the association will likely incur during the period for which the premium is applicable. The premium shall include an amount to cover incurred but not reported losses for the period and may be adjusted for any excess or deficient premiums from previous periods. Excesses or deficiencies from previous periods may be fully adjusted in a single period or may be adjusted over several periods in a manner provided for in the plan of operation. Each member shall be charged an amount equal to that member's total written car years of insurance providing the security required by section 3101(1) or 3103(1), or both, written in this state during the period to which the premium applies, multiplied by the average premium per car. The average premium per car shall be the total premium calculated divided by the total written car years of insurance providing the security required by section 3101(1) or 3103(1) written in this state of all members during the period to which the premium applies. A member shall be charged a premium for a historic vehicle that is insured with the member of 20% of the premium charged for a car insured with the member. As used in this subdivision:

(i) Car includes a motorcycle but does not include a historic vehicle.

(ii) Historic vehicle means a vehicle that is a registered historic vehicle under section 803a or 803p of the

Michigan vehicle code, 1949 PA 300, MCL 257.803a and 257.803p.

(e) Require and accept the payment of premiums from members of the association as provided for in the plan of operation. The association shall do either of the following:

(i) Require payment of the premium in full within 45 days after the premium charge.

(ii) Require payment of the premiums to be made periodically to cover the actual cash obligations of the association.

(f) Receive and distribute all sums required by the operation of the association.

(g) Establish procedures for reviewing claims procedures and practices of members of the association. If the claims procedures or practices of a member are considered inadequate to properly service the liabilities of the association, the association may undertake or may contract with another person, including another member, to adjust or assist in the adjustment of claims for the member on claims that create a potential liability to the association and may charge the cost of the adjustment to the member.

(8) In addition to other powers granted to it by this section, the association may do all of the following:

(a) Sue and be sued in the name of the association. A judgment against the association shall not create any direct liability against the individual members of the association. The association may provide for the indemnification of its members, members of the board of directors of the association, and officers, employees, and other persons lawfully acting on behalf of the association.

(b) Reinsure all or any portion of its potential liability with re-insurers licensed to transact insurance in this state or approved by the commissioner.

(c) Provide for appropriate housing, equipment, and personnel as may be necessary to assure the efficient operation of the association.

(d) Pursuant to the plan of operation, adopt reasonable rules for the administration of the association, enforce those rules, and delegate authority, as the board considers necessary to assure the proper administration and operation of the association consistent with the plan of operation.

(e) Contract for goods and services, including independent claims management, actuarial, investment, and legal services, from others within or without this state to assure the efficient operation of the association.

(f) Hear and determine complaints of a company or other interested party concerning the operation of the association.

(g) Perform other acts not specifically enumerated in this section that are necessary or proper to accomplish the purposes of the association and that are not inconsistent with this section or the plan of operation.

(9) A board of directors is created, hereinafter referred to as the board, which shall be responsible for the operation of the association consistent with the plan of operation and this section.

(10) The plan of operation shall provide for all of the following:

(a) The establishment of necessary facilities.

(b) The management and operation of the association.

(c) Procedures to be utilized in charging premiums, including adjustments from excess or deficient premiums from prior periods.

(d) Procedures governing the actual payment of premiums to the association.

(e) Reimbursement of each member of the board by the association for actual and necessary expenses incurred on association business.

(f) The investment policy of the association.

(g) Any other matters required by or necessary to effectively implement this section.

(11) Each board shall include members that would contribute a total of not less than 40% of the total premium calculated pursuant to subsection (7)(d). Each

director shall be entitled to 1 vote. The initial term of office of a director shall be 2 years.

(12) As part of the plan of operation, the board shall adopt rules providing for the composition and term of successor boards to the initial board, consistent with the membership composition requirements in subsections (11) and (13). Terms of the directors shall be staggered so that the terms of all the directors do not expire at the same time and so that a director does not serve a term of more than 4 years.

(13) The board shall consist of 5 directors, and the commissioner shall be an ex officio member of the board without vote.

(14) Each director shall be appointed by the commissioner and shall serve until that member's successor is selected and qualified. The chairperson of the board shall be elected by the board. A vacancy on the board shall be filled by the commissioner consistent with the plan of operation.

(15) After the board is appointed, the board shall meet as often as the chairperson, the commissioner, or the plan of operation shall require, or at the request of any 3 members of the board. The chairperson shall retain the right to vote on all issues. Four members of the board constitute a quorum.

(16) An annual report of the operations of the association in a form and detail as may be determined by the board shall be furnished to each member.

(17) Not more than 60 days after the initial organizational meeting of the board, the board shall submit to the commissioner for approval a proposed plan of operation consistent with the objectives and provisions of this section, which shall provide for the economical, fair, and nondiscriminatory administration of the association and for the prompt and efficient provision of indemnity. If a plan is not submitted within this 60-day period, then the commissioner, after consultation with the board, shall formulate and place into effect a plan consistent with this section.

(18) The plan of operation, unless approved sooner in writing, shall be considered to meet the requirements of this section if it is not disapproved by written order of the commissioner within 30 days after the date of its submission. Before disapproval of all or any part of the proposed plan of operation, the commissioner shall notify the board in what respect the plan of operation fails to meet the requirements and objectives of this section. If the board fails to submit a revised plan of operation that meets the requirements and objectives of this section within the 30-day period, the commissioner shall enter an order accordingly and shall immediately formulate and place into effect a plan consistent with the requirements and objectives of this section.

(19) The proposed plan of operation or amendments to the plan of operation are subject to majority approval by the board, ratified by a majority of the membership having a vote, with voting rights being apportioned according to the premiums charged in subsection (7)(d) and are subject to approval by the commissioner.

(20) Upon approval by the commissioner and ratification by the members of the plan submitted, or upon the promulgation of a plan by the commissioner, each insurer authorized to write insurance providing the security required by section 3101(1) in this state, as provided in this section, is bound by and shall formally subscribe to and participate in the plan approved as a condition of maintaining its authority to transact insurance in this state.

(21) The association is subject to all the reporting, loss reserve, and investment requirements of the commissioner to the same extent as would a member of the association.

(22) Premiums charged members by the association shall be recognized in the rate-making procedures for insurance rates in the same manner that expenses and premium taxes are recognized.

(23) The commissioner or an authorized representative of the commissioner may visit the association at any time and examine any and all the association's affairs.

(24) The association does not have liability for losses occurring before July 1, 1978.

(25) As used in this section:

(a) Consumer price index means the percentage of change in the consumer price index for all urban consumers in the United States city average for all items for the 24 months prior to October 1 of the year prior to the July 1 effective date of the biennial adjustment under subsection (2)(k) as reported by the United States department of labor, bureau of labor statistics, and as certified by the commissioner.

(b) Motor vehicle accident policy means a policy providing the coverage required under section 3101(1).

(c) Ultimate loss means the actual loss amounts that a member is obligated to pay and that are paid or payable by the member, and do not include claim expenses. An ultimate loss is incurred by the association on the date that the loss occurs.

**History:** Add. 1978, Act 136, Eff. July 1, 1978 ;-- Am. 1980, Act 445, Imd. Eff. Jan. 15, 1981 ;-- Am. 2001, Act 3, Eff. July 1, 2002 ;-- Am. 2002, Act 662, Eff. July 1, 2003

**Compiler's Notes:** Act 143 of 1993, which amended this section, was submitted to the people by referendum petition (as Proposal C) and rejected by a majority of the votes cast at the November 8, 1994, general election.

**Popular Name:** Act 218

**Popular Name:** Essential Insurance

**Popular Name:** No-Fault Insurance

# THE INSURANCE CODE OF 1956 (EXCERPT)

## Act 218 of 1956

**500.3105 Insurer liable for personal protection benefits without regard to fault; bodily injury and accidental bodily injury defined.**

Sec. 3105.

(1) Under personal protection insurance an insurer is liable to pay benefits for accidental bodily injury arising out of the ownership, operation, maintenance or use of a motor vehicle as a motor vehicle, subject to the provisions of this chapter.

(2) Personal protection insurance benefits are due under this chapter without regard to fault.

(3) Bodily injury includes death resulting there from and damage to or loss of a person's prosthetic devices in connection with the injury.

(4) Bodily injury is accidental as to a person claiming personal protection insurance benefits unless suffered intentionally by the injured person or caused intentionally by the claimant. Even though a person knows that bodily injury is substantially certain to be caused by his act or omission, he does not cause or suffer injury intentionally if he acts or refrains from acting for the purpose of averting injury to property or to any person including himself.

*John Gwynne Prosser II*

**History:** Add. 1972, Act 294, Eff. Mar. 30, 1973

**Popular Name:** Act 218

**Popular Name:** Essential Insurance

**Popular Name:** No-Fault Insurance

Â© 2004 Legislative Council, State of Michigan

## THE INSURANCE CODE OF 1956 (EXCERPT)

### Act 218 of 1956

**500.3106 Accidental bodily injury arising out of ownership, operation, maintenance, or use of parked vehicle as motor vehicle; conditions.**

Sec. 3106.

(1) Accidental bodily injury does not arise out of the ownership, operation, maintenance, or use of a parked vehicle as a motor vehicle unless any of the following occur:

(a) The vehicle was parked in such a way as to cause unreasonable risk of the bodily injury which occurred.

(b) Except as provided in subsection (2), the injury was a direct result of physical contact with equipment permanently mounted on the vehicle, while the equipment was being operated or used, or property being lifted onto or lowered from the vehicle in the loading or unloading process.

(c) Except as provided in subsection (2), the injury was sustained by a person while occupying, entering into, or alighting from the vehicle.

(2) Accidental bodily injury does not arise out of the ownership, operation, maintenance, or use of a parked vehicle as a motor vehicle if benefits under the worker's disability compensation act of 1969, Act No. 317 of the Public Acts of 1969, as amended, being sections

418.101 to 418.941 of the Michigan Compiled Laws, or under a similar law of another state or under a similar federal law, are available to an employee who sustains the injury in the course of his or her employment while doing either of the following:

(a) Loading, unloading, or doing mechanical work on a vehicle unless the injury arose from the use or operation of another vehicle. As used in this subdivision, another vehicle does not include a motor vehicle being loaded on, unloaded from, or secured to, as cargo or freight, a motor vehicle.

(b) Entering into or alighting from the vehicle unless the injury was sustained while entering into or alighting from the vehicle immediately after the vehicle became disabled. This subdivision shall not apply if the injury arose from the use or operation of another vehicle. As used in this subdivision, another vehicle does not include a motor vehicle being loaded on, unloaded from or secured to, as cargo or freight, a motor vehicle.

**History:** Add. 1972, Act 294, Eff. Mar. 30, 1973 ;-- Am. 1981, Act 209, Eff. Jan. 1, 1982 ;-- Am. 1986, Act 318, Eff. June 1, 1987

**Compiler's Notes:** Section 2 of Act 209 of 1981 provides: This amendatory act shall take effect January 1, 1982 and shall be applicable to all causes of action which occur after the effective date of this amendatory act.

**Popular Name:** Act 218

**Popular Name:** Essential Insurance

**Popular Name:** No-Fault Insurance

## THE INSURANCE CODE OF 1956 (EXCERPT)

### Act 218 of 1956

**500.3107 Expenses and work loss for which personal protection benefits payable.**

Sec. 3107.

(1) Except as provided in subsection (2), personal protection insurance benefits are payable for the following:

(a) Allowable expenses consisting of all reasonable charges incurred for reasonably necessary products, services and accommodations for an injured person's care, recovery, or rehabilitation. Allowable expenses within personal protection insurance coverage shall not include charges for a hospital room in excess of a reasonable and customary charge for semiprivate accommodations except if the injured person requires special or intensive care, or for funeral and burial expenses in the amount set forth in the policy which shall not be less than $1,750.00 or more than $5,000.00.

(b) Work loss consisting of loss of income from work an injured person would have performed during the first 3 years after the date of the accident if he or she had not been injured. Work loss does not include any loss after the date on which the injured person dies. Because the benefits received from personal protection insurance for loss of income are not taxable income, the benefits payable for such loss of income shall be reduced 15% unless the claimant presents to the insurer in support of his or her claim reasonable proof of a lower value of the income tax advantage in his or her case, in which case the lower value shall apply. Beginning March 30, 1973, the benefits payable for work loss sustained in a single 30-day period and the income earned by an injured person for work during the same period together shall not exceed $1,000.00, which maximum shall apply pro rata to any lesser period of work loss. Beginning October 1, 1974, the maximum shall be adjusted annually to reflect changes in the cost of living under rules prescribed by the commissioner but any change in the maximum shall apply only to benefits arising out of accidents occurring subsequent to the date of change in the maximum.

(c) Expenses not exceeding $20.00 per day, reasonably incurred in obtaining ordinary and necessary services in lieu of those that, if he or she had not been injured, an injured person would have performed during the first 3 years after the date of the accident, not for income but for the benefit of himself or herself or of his or her dependent.

(2) A person who is 60 years of age or older and in the event of an accidental bodily injury would not be eligible to receive work loss benefits under subsection (1)(b) may waive coverage for work loss benefits by signing a waiver on a form provided by the insurer. An insurer shall offer a reduced premium rate to a person who waives coverage under this subsection for work loss benefits. Waiver of coverage for work loss benefits

applies only to work loss benefits payable to the person
or persons who have signed the waiver form.

**History:** Add. 1972, Act 294, Eff. Mar. 30, 1973 ;-- Am. 1988,
Act 312, Eff. Mar. 30, 1989 ;-- Am. 1991, Act 191, Eff. Jan. 1,
1992

**Constitutionality:** The legislature did not violate constitutional
due process or equal protection in providing for cost-of-living
increases for no-fault insurance work loss benefits under
subdivision (b) of this section, but not for no-fault insurance
survivors' loss benefits under S 500.3108. Davey v. Detroit
Automobile Inter-Insurance Exchange, 414 Mich. 1, 322 N.W.2d
541 (1982).

**Compiler's Notes:** Act 143 of 1993, which amended this section,
was submitted to the people by referendum petition (as Proposal
C) and rejected by a majority of the votes cast at the November 8,
1994, general election.

**Popular Name:** Act 218

**Popular Name:** Essential Insurance

**Popular Name:** No-Fault Insurance

**Admin Rule:** R 500.811 of the Michigan Administrative Code.

© 2004 Legislative Council, State of Michigan

# THE INSURANCE CODE OF 1956 (EXCERPT)

## Act 218 of 1956

**500.3107a Basis of work loss for certain injured persons.**

Sec. 3107a.

Subject to the provisions of section 3107(1)(b), work loss for an injured person who is temporarily unemployed at the time of the accident or during the period of disability shall be based on earned income for the last month employed full time preceding the accident.

**History:** Add. 1975, Act 311, Imd. Eff. Dec. 22, 1975 ;-- Am. 1991, Act 191, Eff. Jan. 1, 1992

**Popular Name:** Act 218

**Popular Name:** Essential Insurance

**Popular Name:** No-Fault Insurance

# THE INSURANCE CODE OF 1956 (EXCERPT)

## Act 218 of 1956

**500.3107b Reimbursement or coverage for certain expenses not required; conditional effective date of subdivision (b).**

Sec. 3107b.

Reimbursement or coverage for expenses within personal protection insurance coverage under section 3107 is not required for either of the following:

(a) A practice of optometric service, unless that service was included in the definition of practice of optometry under section 17401 of the public health code, Act No. 368 of the Public Acts of 1978, being section 333.17401 of the Michigan Compiled Laws, as of May 20, 1992.

(b) The use of therapeutic sound or electricity, or both, for the reduction or correction of spinal subluxations in a chiropractic service. This subdivision shall not take effect unless Senate Bill No. 493 of the 87th Legislature is enacted into law.

**History:** Add. 1994, Act 438, Eff. Mar. 30, 1995
**Compiler's Notes:** Senate Bill No. 493 was not enacted into law by the 87th Legislature.

**Popular Name:** Act 218

**Popular Name:** Essential Insurance

**Popular Name:** No-Fault Insurance

Â© 2004 Legislative Council, State of Michigan

# THE INSURANCE CODE OF 1956 (EXCERPT)

## Act 218 of 1956

### 500.3108 Survivor's loss; benefits.

Sec. 3108.

(1) Except as provided in subsection (2), personal protection insurance benefits are payable for a survivor's loss which consists of a loss, after the date on which the deceased died, of contributions of tangible things of economic value, not including services, that dependents of the deceased at the time of the deceased's death would have received for support during their dependency from the deceased if the deceased had not suffered the accidental bodily injury causing death and expenses, not exceeding $20.00 per day, reasonably incurred by these dependents during their dependency and after the date on which the deceased died in obtaining ordinary and necessary services in lieu of those that the deceased would have performed for their benefit if the deceased had not suffered the injury causing death. Except as provided in section (2) the benefits payable for a survivors' loss in connection with the death of a person in a single 30-day period shall not exceed $1,000.00 for accidents occurring before October 1, 1978, and shall not exceed $1,475.00 for accidents occurring on or after October 1, 1978, and is not payable beyond the first three years after the date of the accident.

(2) The maximum payable shall be adjusted annually to reflect changes in the cost of living under rules prescribed by the commissioner. A change in the maximum shall apply only to benefits arising out of accidents occurring subsequent to the date of change in the maximum. The maximum shall apply to the aggregate benefits for all survivors payable under this section on account of the death of any one person.

**History:** Add. 1972, Act 294, Eff. Mar. 30, 1973 ;-- Am. 1978, Act 459, Imd. Eff. Oct. 16, 1978

**Constitutionality:** The legislature did not violate constitutional due process or equal protection in providing for cost-of-living increases for no-fault insurance work loss benefits under §500.3107(b), but not for no-fault insurance survivors' loss benefits under this section. Davey v. Detroit Automobile Inter-Insurance Exchange, 414 Mich. 1, 322 N.W.2d 541 (1982).

**Popular Name:** Act 218

**Popular Name:** Essential Insurance

**Popular Name:** No-Fault Insurance

© 2004 Legislative Council, State of Michigan

# THE INSURANCE CODE OF 1956 (EXCERPT)

## Act 218 of 1956

**500.3109 Subtraction of other benefits from personal protection benefits; injured person defined; deductible provision.**

Sec. 3109.

(1) Benefits provided or required to be provided under the laws of any state or the federal government shall be subtracted from the personal protection insurance benefits otherwise payable for the injury.

(2) An injured person is a natural person suffering accidental bodily injury.

(3) An insurer providing personal protection insurance benefits may offer, at appropriately reduced premium rates, a deductible of a specified dollar amount which does not exceed $300.00 per accident. This deductible may be applicable to all or any specified types of personal protection insurance benefits but shall apply only to benefits payable to the person named in the policy, his spouse and any relative of either domiciled in the same household. Any other deductible provisions require the prior approval of the commissioner.

**History:** Add. 1972, Act 294, Eff. Mar. 30, 1973

**Constitutionality:** In O'Donnel v. State Farm Mutual Automobile Insurance Company, 404 Mich. 524, 273 N.W.2d 829 (1979), the Michigan supreme court held that 500.3109(1) does not violate the due process clause or the equal protection clause of the state or federal constitutions. In Underhill v. Safeco Insurance Company, 407 Mich. 175, 284 N.W.2d 463 (1979), the Michigan supreme court held that subsection (3) of this section authorizing the commissioner to approve deductibles was not an unconstitutional delegation of authority. The Michigan supreme court in Mathis v. Interstate Motor Freight System, 408 Mich. 164, 289 N.W.2d 708 (1980), held that 500.3109(1) as applied to workers' compensation benefits is sustainable under the equal protection clause of the Michigan constitution.

**Popular Name:** Act 218

**Popular Name:** Essential Insurance

**Popular Name:** No-Fault Insurance

Â© 2004 Legislative Council, State of Michigan

# THE INSURANCE CODE OF 1956 (EXCERPT)
## Act 218 of 1956

**500.3109a Offering deductibles and exclusions reasonably related to other health and accident coverage; rates; approval; applicability.**

Sec. 3109a.

An insurer providing personal protection insurance benefits shall offer, at appropriately reduced premium rates, deductibles and exclusions reasonably related to other health and accident coverage on the insured. The deductibles and exclusions required to be offered by this section shall be subject to prior approval by the commissioner and shall apply only to benefits payable to the person named in the policy, the spouse of the insured and any relative of either domiciled in the same household.

**History:** Add. 1974, Act 72, Eff. June 4, 1974

**Constitutionality:** In O'Donnel v. State Farm Mutual Automobile Insurance Company, 404 Mich. 524, 273 N.W.2d 829 (1979), the Michigan supreme court declared this statute constitutional.

**Compiler's Notes:** Act 143 of 1993, which amended this section, was submitted to the people by referendum petition (as Proposal C) and rejected by a majority of the votes cast at the November 8, 1994, general election.

**Popular Name:** Act 218

**Popular Name:** Essential Insurance

**Popular Name:** No-Fault Insurance

Â© 2004 Legislative Council, State of Michigan

## THE INSURANCE CODE OF 1956 (EXCERPT)
## Act 218 of 1956

**500.3110 Dependents of deceased person; termination of dependency; accrual of personal protection benefits.**

Sec. 3110.

(1) The following persons are conclusively presumed to be dependents of a deceased person:

(a) A wife is dependent on a husband with whom she lives at the time of his death.

(b) A husband is dependent on a wife with whom he lives at the time of her death.

(c) A child while under the age of 18 years, or over that age but physically or mentally incapacitated from earning, is dependent on the parent with whom he lives or from whom he receives support regularly at the time of the death of the parent.

(2) In all other cases, questions of dependency and the extent of dependency shall be determined in accordance with the facts as they exist at the time of death.

(3) The dependency of a surviving spouse terminates upon death or remarriage. The dependency of any other person terminates upon the death of the person and continues only so long as the person is under the age of 18 years, physically or mentally incapacitated

from earning, or engaged full time in a formal program of academic or vocational education or training.

(4) Personal protection insurance benefits payable for accidental bodily injury accrue not when the injury occurs but as the allowable expense, work loss or survivors' loss is incurred.

**History:** Add. 1972, Act 294, Eff. Mar. 30, 1973

**Popular Name:** Act 218

**Popular Name:** Essential Insurance

**Popular Name:** No-Fault Insurance

Â© 2004 Legislative Council, State of Michigan

# THE INSURANCE CODE OF 1956 (EXCERPT)

## Act 218 of 1956

### 500.3111 Payment of personal protection benefits for accident occurring out of state.

Sec. 3111.

Personal protection insurance benefits are payable for accidental bodily injury suffered in an accident occurring out of this state, if the accident occurs within the United States, its territories and possessions or in Canada, and the person whose injury is the basis of the claim was at the time of the accident a named insured under a personal protection insurance policy, his spouse, a relative of either domiciled in the same household or an occupant of a vehicle involved in the accident whose owner or registrant was insured under a personal protection insurance policy or has provided security approved by the secretary of state under subsection (4) of section 3101.

**History:** Add. 1972, Act 294, Eff. Mar. 30, 1973

**Popular Name:** Act 218

**Popular Name:** Essential Insurance

**Popular Name:** No-Fault Insurance

Â© 2004 Legislative Council, State of Michigan

# THE INSURANCE CODE OF 1956 (EXCERPT)
## Act 218 of 1956

## 500.3112 Persons to whom personal protection benefits payable; discharge of insurer's liability.

Sec. 3112.

Personal protection insurance benefits are payable to or for the benefit of an injured person or, in case of his death, to or for the benefit of his dependents. Payment by an insurer in good faith of personal protection insurance benefits, to or for the benefit of a person who it believes is entitled to the benefits, discharges the insurer's liability to the extent of the payments unless the insurer has been notified in writing of the claim of some other person. If there is doubt about the proper person to receive the benefits or the proper apportionment among the persons entitled thereto, the insurer, the claimant or any other interested person may apply to the circuit court for an appropriate order. The court may designate the payees and make an equitable apportionment, taking into account the relationship of the payees to the injured person and other factors as the court considers appropriate. In the absence of a court order directing otherwise the insurer may pay:

(a) To the dependents of the injured person, the personal protection insurance benefits accrued before his death without appointment of an administrator or executor.

(b) To the surviving spouse, the personal protection insurance benefits due any dependent children living with the spouse.

**History:** Add. 1972, Act 294, Eff. Mar. 30, 1973

**Popular Name:** Act 218

**Popular Name:** Essential Insurance

**Popular Name:** No-Fault Insurance

Â© 2004 Legislative Council, State of Michigan

# THE INSURANCE CODE OF 1956 (EXCERPT)
## Act 218 of 1956

**500.3113 Persons not entitled to personal protection benefits.**

Sec. 3113.

A person is not entitled to be paid personal protection insurance benefits for accidental bodily injury if at the time of the accident any of the following circumstances existed:

(a) The person was using a motor vehicle or motorcycle which he or she had taken unlawfully, unless the person reasonably believed that he or she was entitled to take and use the vehicle.

(b) The person was the owner or registrant of a motor vehicle or motorcycle involved in the accident with respect to which the security required by section 3101 or 3103 was not in effect.

(c) The person was not a resident of this state, was an occupant of a motor vehicle or motorcycle not registered in this state, and was not insured by an insurer which has filed a certification in compliance with section 3163.

**History:** Add. 1972, Act 294, Eff. Mar. 30, 1973 ;-- Am. 1986, Act 93, Eff. July 8, 1986

**Compiler's Notes:** Section 2 of Act 93 of 1986 provides: â€œThis amendatory act shall not apply to causes of action arising before the effective date of this amendatory act.â€

**Popular Name:** Act 218

**Popular Name:** Essential Insurance

**Popular Name:** No-Fault Insurance

Â© 2004 Legislative Council, State of Michigan

# THE INSURANCE CODE OF 1956 (EXCERPT)

## Act 218 of 1956

**500.3114 Persons entitled to personal protection insurance benefits or personal injury benefits; recoupment barred; order of priority for claim of motor vehicle occupant or motorcycle operator or passenger; 2 or more insurers in same order of priority; partial recoupment.**

Sec. 3114.

(1) Except as provided in subsections (2), (3), and (5), a personal protection insurance policy described in section 3101(1) applies to accidental bodily injury to the person named in the policy, the person's spouse, and a relative of either domiciled in the same household, if the injury arises from a motor vehicle accident. A personal injury insurance policy described in section 3103(2) applies to accidental bodily injury to the person named in the policy, the person's spouse, and a relative of either domiciled in the same household, if the injury arises from a motorcycle accident. When personal protection insurance benefits or personal injury benefits described in section 3103(2) are payable to or for the benefit of an injured person under his or her own policy and would also be payable under the policy of his or her spouse, relative, or relative's spouse, the injured person's insurer shall pay all of the benefits and is not entitled to recoupment from the other insurer.

(2) A person suffering accidental bodily injury while an operator or a passenger of a motor vehicle operated in the business of transporting passengers shall receive the personal protection insurance benefits to which the person is entitled from the insurer of the motor vehicle. This subsection does not apply to a passenger in the following, unless that passenger is not entitled to personal protection insurance benefits under any other policy:

(a) A school bus, as defined by the department of education, providing transportation not prohibited by law.

(b) A bus operated by a common carrier of passengers certified by the department of transportation.

(c) A bus operating under a government sponsored transportation program.

(d) A bus operated by or providing service to a nonprofit organization.

(e) A taxicab insured as prescribed in section 3101 or 3102.

(f) A bus operated by a canoe or other watercraft, bicycle, or horse livery used only to transport passengers to or from a destination point.

(3) An employee, his or her spouse, or a relative of either domiciled in the same household, who suffers accidental bodily injury while an occupant of a motor vehicle owned or registered by the employer, shall receive personal protection insurance benefits to

which the employee is entitled from the insurer of the furnished vehicle.

(4) Except as provided in subsections (1) to (3), a person suffering accidental bodily injury arising from a motor vehicle accident while an occupant of a motor vehicle shall claim personal protection insurance benefits from insurers in the following order of priority:

(a) The insurer of the owner or registrant of the vehicle occupied.

(b) The insurer of the operator of the vehicle occupied.

(5) A person suffering accidental bodily injury arising from a motor vehicle accident which shows evidence of the involvement of a motor vehicle while an operator or passenger of a motorcycle shall claim personal protection insurance benefits from insurers in the following order of priority:

(a) The insurer of the owner or registrant of the motor vehicle involved in the accident.

(b) The insurer of the operator of the motor vehicle involved in the accident.

(c) The motor vehicle insurer of the operator of the motorcycle involved in the accident.

(d) The motor vehicle insurer of the owner or registrant of the motorcycle involved in the accident.

(6) If 2 or more insurers are in the same order of priority to provide personal protection insurance benefits under subsection (5), an insurer paying benefits due is entitled to partial recoupment from the other insurers in the same order of priority, together with a reasonable amount of partial recoupment of the expense of processing the claim, in order to accomplish equitable distribution of the loss among all of the insurers.

**History:** Add. 1972, Act 294, Eff. Mar. 30, 1973 ;-- Am. 1975, Act 137, Imd. Eff. July 3, 1975 ;-- Am. 1976, Act 356, Imd. Eff. Dec. 21, 1976 ;-- Am. 1977, Act 53, Imd. Eff. July 5, 1977 ;-- Am. 1980, Act 445, Imd. Eff. Jan. 15, 1981 ;-- Am. 1984, Act 372, Imd. Eff. Dec. 27, 1984 ;-- Am. 2002, Act 38, Imd. Eff. Mar. 7, 2002

**Popular Name:** Act 218

**Popular Name:** Essential Insurance

**Popular Name:** No-Fault Insurance

# THE INSURANCE CODE OF 1956 (EXCERPT)

## Act 218 of 1956

## 500.3115 Priorities as to claims of persons not occupants of vehicle; partial recoupment; limitation on benefits.

Sec. 3115.

(1) Except as provided in subsection (1) of section 3114, a person suffering accidental bodily injury while not an occupant of a motor vehicle shall claim personal protection insurance benefits from insurers in the following order of priority:

(a) Insurers of owners or registrants of motor vehicles involved in the accident.

(b) Insurers of operators of motor vehicles involved in the accident.

(2) When 2 or more insurers are in the same order of priority to provide personal protection insurance benefits an insurer paying benefits due is entitled to partial recoupment from the other insurers in the same order of priority, together with a reasonable amount of partial recoupment of the expense of processing the claim, in order to accomplish equitable distribution of the loss among such insurers.

(3) A limit upon the amount of personal protection insurance benefits available because of accidental bodily injury to 1 person arising from 1 motor vehicle

accident shall be determined without regard to the number of policies applicable to the accident.

**History:** Add. 1972, Act 294, Eff. Mar. 30, 1973

**Constitutionality:** The legislative scheme which allows motorcyclists to receive no-fault benefits for personal injuries without requiring them to maintain no-fault security does not deny automobile drivers equal protection or due process of law. Underhill v. Safeco Insurance Company, 407 Mich. 175, 284 N.W.2d 463 (1979).

**Compiler's Notes:** Act 143 of 1993, which amended this section, was submitted to the people by referendum petition (as Proposal C) and rejected by a majority of the votes cast at the November 8, 1994, general election.

**Popular Name:** Act 218

**Popular Name:** Essential Insurance

**Popular Name:** No-Fault Insurance

Â© 2004 Legislative Council, State of Michigan

# THE INSURANCE CODE OF 1956 (EXCERPT)

## Act 218 of 1956

**500.3116 Value of claim in tort; subtraction from or reimbursement for benefits.**

Sec. 3116.

(1) A subtraction from personal protection insurance benefits shall not be made because of the value of a claim in tort based on the same accidental bodily injury.

(2) A subtraction from or reimbursement for personal protection insurance benefits paid or payable under this chapter shall be made only if recovery is realized upon a tort claim arising from an accident occurring outside this state, a tort claim brought within this state against the owner or operator of a motor vehicle with respect to which the security required by section 3101 (3) and (4) was not in effect, or a tort claim brought within this state based on intentionally caused harm to persons or property, and shall be made only to the extent that the recovery realized by the claimant is for damages for which the claimant has received or would otherwise be entitled to receive personal protection insurance benefits. A subtraction shall be made only to the extent of the recovery, exclusive of reasonable attorneys' fees and other reasonable expenses incurred in effecting the recovery. If personal protection insurance benefits have already been received, the claimant shall repay to the insurers out of the recovery a sum equal to the benefits

received, but not more than the recovery exclusive of reasonable attorneys' fees and other reasonable expenses incurred in effecting the recovery. The insurer shall have a lien on the recovery to this extent. A recovery by an injured person or his or her estate for loss suffered by the person shall not be subtracted in calculating benefits due a dependent after the death and a recovery by a dependent for loss suffered by the dependent after the death shall not be subtracted in calculating benefits due the injured person.

(3) A personal protection insurer with a right of reimbursement under subsection (1), if suffering loss from inability to collect reimbursement out of a payment received by a claimant upon a tort claim is entitled to indemnity from a person who, with notice of the insurer's interest, made the payment to the claimant without making the claimant and the insurer joint payees as their interests may appear or without obtaining the insurer's consent to a different method of payment.

(4) A subtraction or reimbursement shall not be due the claimant's insurer from that portion of any recovery to the extent that recovery is realized for noneconomic loss as provided in section 3135(1) and (2)(b) or for allowable expenses, work loss, and survivor's loss as defined in sections 3107 to 3110 in excess of the amount recovered by the claimant from his or her insurer.

**History:** Add. 1972, Act 294, Eff. Mar. 30, 1973 ;-- Am. 1978, Act 461, Imd. Eff. Oct. 16, 1978

**Compiler's Notes:** Act 143 of 1993, which amended this section, was submitted to the people by referendum petition (as Proposal C) and rejected by a majority of the votes cast at the November 8, 1994, general election.

**Popular Name:** Act 218

**Popular Name:** Essential Insurance

**Popular Name:** No-Fault Insurance

Â© 2004 Legislative Council, State of Michigan

# THE INSURANCE CODE OF 1956 (EXCERPT)

## Act 218 of 1956

### 500.3121 Liability for accidental damage to tangible property.

Sec. 3121.

(1) Under property protection insurance an insurer is liable to pay benefits for accidental damage to tangible property arising out of the ownership, operation, maintenance, or use of a motor vehicle as a motor vehicle subject to the provisions of this section and sections 3123, 3125, and 3127. However, accidental damage to tangible property does not include accidental damage to tangible property, other than the insured motor vehicle, that occurs within the course of a business of repairing, servicing, or otherwise maintaining motor vehicles.

(2) Property protection insurance benefits are due under the conditions stated in this chapter without regard to fault.

(3) Damage to tangible property consists of physical injury to or destruction of the property and loss of use of the property so injured or destroyed.

(4) Damage to tangible property is accidental, as to a person claiming property protection insurance benefits, unless it is suffered or caused intentionally by the claimant. Even though a person knows that damage to tangible property is substantially certain to be caused

by his or her act or omission, he or she does not cause or suffer such damage intentionally if he or she acts or refrains from acting for the purpose of averting injury to any person, including himself or herself, or for the purpose of averting damage to tangible property.

(5) Property protection insurance benefits consist of the lesser of reasonable repair costs or replacement costs less depreciation and, if applicable, the value of loss of use. However, property protection insurance benefits paid under 1 policy for damage to all tangible property arising from 1 accident shall not exceed $1,000,000.00.

**History:** Add. 1972, Act 294, Eff. Mar. 30, 1973 ;-- Am. 1993, Act 290, Imd. Eff. Dec. 28, 1993

**Popular Name:** Act 218

**Popular Name:** Essential Insurance

**Popular Name:** No-Fault Insurance

Â© 2004 Legislative Council, State of Michigan

## THE INSURANCE CODE OF 1956 (EXCERPT)

### Act 218 of 1956

**500.3123 Exclusions from property protection insurance benefits.**

Sec. 3123.

(1) Damage to the following kinds of property is excluded from property protection insurance benefits:

(a) Vehicles and their contents, including trailers, operated or designed for operation upon a public highway by power other than muscular power, unless the vehicle is parked in a manner as not to cause unreasonable risk of the damage which occurred.

(b) Property owned by a person named in a property protection insurance policy, the person's spouse or a relative of either domiciled in the same household, if the person named, the person's spouse, or the relative was the owner, registrant, or operator of a vehicle involved in the motor vehicle accident out of which the property damage arose.

(2) Property protection insurance benefits are not payable for property damage arising from motor vehicle accidents occurring outside the state.

(3) Property protection insurance benefits are not payable for property damage to utility transmission lines, wires, or cables arising from the failure of a municipality, utility company, or cable television

company to comply with the requirements of section 16 of Act No. 368 of the Public Acts of 1925, being section 247.186 of the Michigan Compiled Laws.

**History:** Add. 1972, Act 294, Eff. Mar. 30, 1973 ;-- Am. 1978, Act 65, Imd. Eff. Mar. 14, 1978

**Popular Name:** Act 218

**Popular Name:** Essential Insurance

**Popular Name:** No-Fault Insurance

Â© 2004 Legislative Council, State of Michigan

# THE INSURANCE CODE OF 1956 (EXCERPT)

## Act 218 of 1956

## 500.3125 Priorities in claiming property protection benefits.

Sec. 3125.

A person suffering accidental property damage shall claim property protection insurance benefits from insurers in the following order of priority: insurers of owners or registrants of vehicles involved in the accident; and insurers of operators of vehicles involved in the accident.

**History:** Add. 1972, Act 294, Eff. Mar. 30, 1973

**Popular Name:** Act 218

**Popular Name:** Essential Insurance

**Popular Name:** No-Fault Insurance

Â© 2004 Legislative Council, State of Michigan

# THE INSURANCE CODE OF 1956 (EXCERPT)

## Act 218 of 1956

**500.3127 Distribution of loss, reimbursement, and indemnification among property protection insurers.**

Sec. 3127.

The provisions for distribution of loss and for reimbursement and indemnification among personal protection insurers as set forth in subsection (2) of section 3115 and in section 3116 also applies to property protection insurers.

**History:** Add. 1972, Act 294, Eff. Mar. 30, 1973

**Popular Name:** Act 218

**Popular Name:** Essential Insurance

**Popular Name:** No-Fault Insurance

Â© 2004 Legislative Council, State of Michigan

# THE INSURANCE CODE OF 1956 (EXCERPT)

## Act 218 of 1956

### 500.3131 Residual liability insurance; coverage.

Sec. 3131.

(1) Residual liability insurance shall cover bodily injury and property damage which occurs within the United States, its territories and possessions, or in Canada. This insurance shall afford coverage equivalent to that required as evidence of automobile liability insurance under the financial responsibility laws of the place in which the injury or damage occurs. In this state this insurance shall afford coverage for automobile liability retained by section 3135.

(2) This section shall not require coverage in this state other than that required by section 3009(1). This section shall apply to all insurance contracts in force as of October 1, 1973, or entered into after that date.

**History:** Add. 1972, Act 294, Eff. Mar. 30, 1973 ;-- Am. 1978, Act 460, Imd. Eff. Oct. 16, 1978

**Popular Name:** Act 218

**Popular Name:** Essential Insurance

**Popular Name:** No-Fault Insurance

# THE INSURANCE CODE OF 1956 (EXCERPT)

## Act 218 of 1956

**500.3135 Tort liability for non economic loss; action for damages pursuant to subsection (1); abolition of tort liability; exceptions; action for damages pursuant to subsection (3)(d); commencement of action; removal; costs; decision as res judicata; serious impairment of body function defined.**

Sec. 3135.

(1) A person remains subject to tort liability for non economic loss caused by his or her ownership, maintenance, or use of a motor vehicle only if the injured person has suffered death, serious impairment of body function, or permanent serious disfigurement.

(2) For a cause of action for damages pursuant to subsection (1) filed on or after July 26, 1996, all of the following apply:

(a) The issues of whether an injured person has suffered serious impairment of body function or permanent serious disfigurement are questions of law for the court if the court finds either of the following:

(i) There is no factual dispute concerning the nature and extent of the person's injuries.

(ii) There is a factual dispute concerning the nature and extent of the person's injuries, but the dispute is not material to the determination as to whether the person has suffered a serious impairment of body function or permanent serious disfigurement. However, for a closed-head injury, a question of fact for the jury is created if a licensed allopathic or osteopathic physician who regularly diagnoses or treats closed-head injuries testifies under oath that there may be a serious neurological injury.

(b) Damages shall be assessed on the basis of comparative fault, except that damages shall not be assessed in favor of a party who is more than 50% at fault.

(c) Damages shall not be assessed in favor of a party who was operating his or her own vehicle at the time the injury occurred and did not have in effect for that motor vehicle the security required by section 3101 at the time the injury occurred.

(3) Notwithstanding any other provision of law, tort liability arising from the ownership, maintenance, or use within this state of a motor vehicle with respect to which the security required by section 3101 was in effect is abolished except as to:

(a) Intentionally caused harm to persons or property. Even though a person knows that harm to persons or property is substantially certain to be caused by his or her act or omission, the person does not cause or suffer that harm intentionally if he or she acts or refrains from acting for the purpose of averting injury to any person, including himself or herself, or for the purpose of averting damage to tangible property.

(b) Damages for non economic loss as provided and limited in subsections (1) and (2).

(c) Damages for allowable expenses, work loss, and survivor's loss as defined in sections 3107 to 3110 in excess of the daily, monthly, and 3-year limitations contained in those sections. The party liable for damages is entitled to an exemption reducing his or her liability by the amount of taxes that would have been payable on account of income the injured person would have received if he or she had not been injured.

(d) Damages for economic loss by a nonresident in excess of the personal protection insurance benefits provided under section 3163(4). Damages under this subdivision are not recoverable to the extent that benefits covering the same loss are available from other sources, regardless of the nature or number of benefit sources available and regardless of the nature or form of the benefits.

(e) Damages up to $500.00 to motor vehicles, to the extent that the damages are not covered by insurance. An action for damages pursuant to this subdivision shall be conducted in compliance with subsection (4).

(4) In an action for damages pursuant to subsection (3)(e):

(a) Damages shall be assessed on the basis of comparative fault, except that damages shall not be assessed in favor of a party who is more than 50% at fault.

(b) Liability shall not be a component of residual liability, as prescribed in section 3131, for which maintenance of security is required by this act.

(5) Actions under subsection (3)(e) shall be commenced, whenever legally possible, in the small claims division of the district court or the municipal court. If the defendant or plaintiff removes the action to a higher court and does not prevail, the judge may assess costs.

(6) A decision of a court made pursuant to subsection (3)(e) is not res judicata in any proceeding to determine any other liability arising from the same circumstances as gave rise to the action brought pursuant to subsection (3)(e).

(7) As used in this section, serious impairment of body function means an objectively manifested impairment of an important body function that affects the person's general ability to lead his or her normal life.

**History:** Add. 1972, Act 294, Eff. Mar. 30, 1973 ;-- Am. 1979, Act 145, Imd. Eff. Nov. 13, 1979 ;-- Am. 1979, Act 147, Imd. Eff. Nov. 13, 1979 ;-- Am. 1995, Act 222, Eff. Mar. 28, 1996 ;-- Am. 2002, Act 697, Eff. Mar. 31, 2003

**Compiler's Notes:** Act 143 of 1993, which amended this section, was submitted to the people by referendum petition (as Proposal C) and rejected by a majority of the votes cast at the November 8, 1994, general election.

**Popular Name:** Act 218

**Popular Name:** Essential Insurance

**Popular Name:** No-Fault Insurance

# THE INSURANCE CODE OF 1956 (EXCERPT)

## Act 218 of 1956

### 500.3141 Notice of accident.

Sec. 3141.

An insurer may require written notice to be given as soon as practicable after an accident involving a motor vehicle with respect to which the policy affords the security required by this chapter.

**History:** Add. 1972, Act 294, Eff. Mar. 30, 1973

**Popular Name:** Act 218

**Popular Name:** Essential Insurance

**Popular Name:** No-Fault Insurance

Â© 2004 Legislative Council, State of Michigan

# THE INSURANCE CODE OF 1956 (EXCERPT)

## Act 218 of 1956

## 500.3142 Personal protection benefits payable as loss accrues; overdue benefits.

Sec. 3142.

(1) Personal protection insurance benefits are payable as loss accrues.

(2) Personal protection insurance benefits are overdue if not paid within 30 days after an insurer receives reasonable proof of the fact and of the amount of loss sustained. If reasonable proof is not supplied as to the entire claim, the amount supported by reasonable proof is overdue if not paid within 30 days after the proof is received by the insurer. Any part of the remainder of the claim that is later supported by reasonable proof is overdue if not paid within 30 days after the proof is received by the insurer. For the purpose of calculating the extent to which benefits are overdue, payment shall be treated as made on the date a draft or other valid instrument was placed in the United States mail in a properly addressed, postpaid envelope, or, if not so posted, on the date of delivery.

(3) An overdue payment bears simple interest at the rate of 12% per annum.

**History:** Add. 1972, Act 294, Eff. Mar. 30, 1973

**Compiler's Notes:** Act 143 of 1993, which amended this section, was submitted to the people by referendum petition (as Proposal C) and rejected by a majority of the votes cast at the November 8, 1994, general election.

**Popular Name:** Act 218

**Popular Name:** Essential Insurance

**Popular Name:** No-Fault Insurance

Â© 2004 Legislative Council, State of Michigan

# THE INSURANCE CODE OF 1956 (EXCERPT)

## Act 218 of 1956

## 500.3143 Assignment of right to future benefits void.

Sec. 3143.

An agreement for assignment of a right to benefits payable in the future is void.

**History:** Add. 1972, Act 294, Eff. Mar. 30, 1973

**Popular Name:** Act 218

**Popular Name:** Essential Insurance

**Popular Name:** No-Fault Insurance

Â© 2004 Legislative Council, State of Michigan

# THE INSURANCE CODE OF 1956 (EXCERPT)

## Act 218 of 1956

**500.3145 Limitation of actions for recovery of personal or property protection benefits; notice of injury.**

Sec. 3145.

(1) An action for recovery of personal protection insurance benefits payable under this chapter for accidental bodily injury may not be commenced later than 1 year after the date of the accident causing the injury unless written notice of injury as provided herein has been given to the insurer within 1 year after the accident or unless the insurer has previously made a payment of personal protection insurance benefits for the injury. If the notice has been given or a payment has been made, the action may be commenced at any time within 1 year after the most recent allowable expense, work loss or survivor's loss has been incurred. However, the claimant may not recover benefits for any portion of the loss incurred more than 1 year before the date on which the action was commenced. The notice of injury required by this subsection may be given to the insurer or any of its authorized agents by a person claiming to be entitled to benefits therefor, or by someone in his behalf. The notice shall give the name and address of the claimant and indicate in ordinary language the name of the person injured and the time, place and nature of his injury.

(2) An action for recovery of property protection insurance benefits shall not be commenced later than 1 year after the accident.

**History:** Add. 1972, Act 294, Eff. Mar. 30, 1973

**Compiler's Notes:** Act 143 of 1993, which amended this section, was submitted to the people by referendum petition (as Proposal C) and rejected by a majority of the votes cast at the November 8, 1994, general election.

**Popular Name:** Act 218

**Popular Name:** Essential Insurance

**Popular Name:** No-Fault Insurance

Â© 2004 Legislative Council, State of Michigan

# THE INSURANCE CODE OF 1956 (EXCERPT)

## Act 218 of 1956

## 500.3146 Limitation of action by insurer for recovery or indemnity.

Sec. 3146.

An action by an insurer to enforce its rights of recovery or indemnity under section 3116 may not be commenced later than 1 year after payment has been received by a claimant upon a tort claim with respect to which the insurer has a right of reimbursement or recovery under section 3116.

**History:** Add. 1972, Act 294, Eff. Mar. 30, 1973

**Popular Name:** Act 218

**Popular Name:** Essential Insurance

**Popular Name:** No-Fault Insurance

Â© 2004 Legislative Council, State of Michigan

# THE INSURANCE CODE OF 1956 (EXCERPT)

## Act 218 of 1956

**500.3148 Attorney's fee.**

Sec. 3148.

(1) An attorney is entitled to a reasonable fee for advising and representing a claimant in an action for personal or property protection insurance benefits which are overdue. The attorney's fee shall be a charge against the insurer in addition to the benefits recovered, if the court finds that the insurer unreasonably refused to pay the claim or unreasonably delayed in making proper payment.

(2) An insurer may be allowed by a court an award of a reasonable sum against a claimant as an attorney's fee for the insurer's attorney in defense against a claim that was in some respect fraudulent or so excessive as to have no reasonable foundation. To the extent that personal or property protection insurance benefits are then due or thereafter come due to the claimant because of loss resulting from the injury on which the claim is based, such a fee may be treated as an offset against such benefits; also, judgment may be entered against the claimant for any amount of a fee awarded against him and not offset in this way or otherwise paid.

**History:** Add. 1972, Act 294, Eff. Mar. 30, 1973

**Popular Name:** Act 218

**Popular Name:** Essential Insurance

**Popular Name:** No-Fault Insurance

Â© 2004 Legislative Council, State of Michigan

# THE INSURANCE CODE OF 1956 (EXCERPT)

## Act 218 of 1956

**500.3151 Submission to mental or physical examination.**

Sec. 3151.

When the mental or physical condition of a person is material to a claim that has been or may be made for past or future personal protection insurance benefits, the person shall submit to mental or physical examination by physicians. A personal protection insurer may include reasonable provisions in a personal protection insurance policy for mental and physical examination of persons claiming personal protection insurance benefits.

**History:** Add. 1972, Act 294, Eff. Mar. 30, 1973

**Popular Name:** Act 218

**Popular Name:** Essential Insurance

**Popular Name:** No-Fault Insurance

Â© 2004 Legislative Council, State of Michigan

# THE INSURANCE CODE OF 1956 (EXCERPT)

## Act 218 of 1956

**500.3152 Report of mental or physical examination.**

Sec. 3152.

If requested by a person examined, a party causing an examination to be made shall deliver to him a copy of every written report concerning the examination rendered by an examining physician, at least 1 of which reports shall set out his findings and conclusions in detail. After such request and delivery, the party causing the examination to be made is entitled upon request to receive from the person examined every written report available to him or his representative concerning any examination relevant to the claim, previously or thereafter made, of the same mental or physical condition, and the names and addresses of physicians and medical care facilities rendering diagnoses or treatment in regard to the injury or to a relevant past injury, and shall authorize the insurer to inspect and copy records of physicians, hospitals, clinics or other medical facilities relevant to the claim. By requesting and obtaining a report of the examination so ordered or by taking the deposition of the examiner, the person examined waives any privilege he may have, in relation to the claim for benefits, regarding the testimony of every other person who has examined or may thereafter examine him in respect of the same mental or physical condition.

**History:** Add. 1972, Act 294, Eff. Mar. 30, 1973

**Popular Name:** Act 218

**Popular Name:** Essential Insurance

**Popular Name:** No-Fault Insurance

Â© 2004 Legislative Council, State of Michigan

# THE INSURANCE CODE OF 1956 (EXCERPT)

## Act 218 of 1956

### 500.3153 Court orders as to noncompliance with Â§Â§ 500.3151 and 500.3152.

Sec. 3153.

A court may make such orders in regard to the refusal to comply with sections 3151 and 3152 as are just, except that an order shall not be entered directing the arrest of a person for disobeying an order to submit to a physical or mental examination. The orders that may be made in regard to such a refusal include, but are not limited to:

(a) An order that the mental or physical condition of the disobedient person shall be taken to be established for the purposes of the claim in accordance with the contention of the party obtaining the order.

(b) An order refusing to allow the disobedient person to support or oppose designated claims or defenses, or prohibiting him from introducing evidence of mental or physical condition.

(c) An order rendering judgment by default against the disobedient person as to his entire claim or a designated part of it.

(d) An order requiring the disobedient person to reimburse the insurer for reasonable attorneys' fees and expenses incurred in defense against the claim.

(e) An order requiring delivery of a report, in conformity with section 3152, on such terms as are just, and if a physician fails or refuses to make the report a court may exclude his testimony if offered at trial.

**History:** Add. 1972, Act 294, Eff. Mar. 30, 1973

**Popular Name:** Act 218

**Popular Name:** Essential Insurance

**Popular Name:** No-Fault Insurance

Â© 2004 Legislative Council, State of Michigan

# THE INSURANCE CODE OF 1956 (EXCERPT)

## Act 218 of 1956

## 500.3157 Charges for products, services, and accommodations where treatment rendered.

Sec. 3157.

A physician, hospital, clinic or other person or institution lawfully rendering treatment to an injured person for an accidental bodily injury covered by personal protection insurance, and a person or institution providing rehabilitative occupational training following the injury, may charge a reasonable amount for the products, services and accommodations rendered. The charge shall not exceed the amount the person or institution customarily charges for like products, services and accommodations in cases not involving insurance.

**History:** Add. 1972, Act 294, Eff. Mar. 30, 1973

**Compiler's Notes:** Act 143 of 1993, which amended this section, was submitted to the people by referendum petition (as Proposal C) and rejected by a majority of the votes cast at the November 8, 1994, general election.

**Popular Name:** Act 218

**Popular Name:** Essential Insurance

**Popular Name:** No-Fault Insurance

Â© 2004 Legislative Council, State of Michigan

# THE INSURANCE CODE OF 1956 (EXCERPT)

## Act 218 of 1956

### 500.3158 Statement of earnings; report and records from medical institution.

Sec. 3158.

(1) An employer, when a request is made by a personal protection insurer against whom a claim has been made, shall furnish forthwith, in a form approved by the commissioner of insurance, a sworn statement of the earnings since the time of the accidental bodily injury and for a reasonable period before the injury, of the person upon whose injury the claim is based.

(2) A physician, hospital, clinic or other medical institution providing, before or after an accidental bodily injury upon which a claim for personal protection insurance benefits is based, any product, service or accommodation in relation to that or any other injury, or in relation to a condition claimed to be connected with that or any other injury, if requested to do so by the insurer against whom the claim has been made, (a) shall furnish forthwith a written report of the history, condition, treatment and dates and costs of treatment of the injured person and (b) shall produce forthwith and permit inspection and copying of its records regarding the history, condition, treatment and dates and costs of treatment.

**History:** Add. 1972, Act 294, Eff. Mar. 30, 1973

**Popular Name:** Act 218

**Popular Name:** Essential Insurance

**Popular Name:** No-Fault Insurance

# THE INSURANCE CODE OF 1956 (EXCERPT)

## Act 218 of 1956

### 500.3159 Discovery.

Sec. 3159.

In a dispute regarding an insurer's right to discovery of facts about an injured person's earnings or about his history, condition, treatment and dates and costs of treatment, a court may enter an order for the discovery. The order may be made only on motion for good cause shown and upon notice to all persons having an interest, and shall specify the time, place, manner, conditions and scope of the discovery. A court, in order to protect against annoyance, embarrassment or oppression, as justice requires, may enter an order refusing discovery or specifying conditions of discovery and may order payments of costs and expenses of the proceeding, including reasonable fees for the appearance of attorneys at the proceedings, as justice requires.

**History:** Add. 1972, Act 294, Eff. Mar. 30, 1973

**Popular Name:** Act 218

**Popular Name:** Essential Insurance

**Popular Name:** No-Fault Insurance

Â© 2004 Legislative Council, State of Michigan

# THE INSURANCE CODE OF 1956 (EXCERPT)

## Act 218 of 1956

**500.3163 Certification by admitted and non admitted insurers as to protection of out-of-state resident; rights and immunities of insurer and insured; benefits to out-of-state resident; limitation.**

Sec. 3163.

(1) An insurer authorized to transact automobile liability insurance and personal and property protection insurance in this state shall file and maintain a written certification that any accidental bodily injury or property damage occurring in this state arising from the ownership, operation, maintenance, or use of a motor vehicle as a motor vehicle by an out-of-state resident who is insured under its automobile liability insurance policies, is subject to the personal and property protection insurance system under this act.

(2) A non admitted insurer may voluntarily file the certification described in subsection (1).

(3) Except as otherwise provided in subsection (4), if a certification filed under subsection (1) or (2) applies to accidental bodily injury or property damage, the insurer and its insured with respect to that injury or damage have the rights and immunities under this act for personal and property protection insured, and claimants have the rights and benefits of personal and property protection insurance claimants, including the

right to receive benefits from the electing insurer as if it were an insurer of personal and property protection insurance applicable to the accidental bodily injury or property damage.

(4) If an insurer of an out-of-state resident is required to provide benefits under subsections (1) to (3) to that out-of-state resident for accidental bodily injury for an accident in which the out-of-state resident was not an occupant of a motor vehicle registered in this state, the insurer is only liable for the amount of ultimate loss sustained up to $500,000.00. Benefits under this subsection are not recoverable to the extent that benefits covering the same loss are available from other sources, regardless of the nature or number of benefit sources available and regardless of the nature or form of the benefits.

**History:** Add. 1972, Act 294, Eff. Mar. 30, 1973 ;-- Am. 2002, Act 697, Eff. Mar. 31, 2003

**Popular Name:** Act 218

**Popular Name:** Essential Insurance

**Popular Name:** No-Fault Insurance

Â© 2004 Legislative Council, State of Michigan

# THE INSURANCE CODE OF 1956 (EXCERPT)
## Act 218 of 1956

### 500.3171 Assigned claims facility and plan; organization and maintenance; participation; costs; rules.

Sec. 3171.

The secretary of state shall organize and maintain an assigned claims facility and plan. A self-insurer and insurer writing insurance as provided by this chapter in this state shall participate in the assigned claims plan. Costs incurred in the operation of the facility and the plan shall be allocated fairly among insurers and self-insurers. The secretary of state shall promulgate rules to implement the facility and plan in accordance with and subject to Act No. 306 of the Public Acts of 1969, as amended, being sections 24.201 to 24.315 of the Compiled Laws of 1948.

**History:** Add. 1972, Act 294, Eff. Mar. 30, 1973 ;-- Am. 1972, Act 345, Imd. Eff. Jan. 9, 1973

**Popular Name:** Act 218

**Popular Name:** Essential Insurance

**Popular Name:** No-Fault Insurance

**Admin Rule:** R 11.101 et seq. of the Michigan Administrative Code.

# THE INSURANCE CODE OF 1956 (EXCERPT)

## Act 218 of 1956

**500.3172 Conditions to obtaining personal protection insurance benefits through assigned claims plan; collection of unpaid benefits; reimbursement from defaulting insurers; reduction of benefits; applicability of subsection (2); definitions; effect of dispute between insurers.**

Sec. 3172.

(1) A person entitled to claim because of accidental bodily injury arising out of the ownership, operation, maintenance, or use of a motor vehicle as a motor vehicle in this state may obtain personal protection insurance benefits through an assigned claims plan if no personal protection insurance is applicable to the injury, no personal protection insurance applicable to the injury can be identified, the personal protection insurance applicable to the injury cannot be ascertained because of a dispute between 2 or more automobile insurers concerning their obligation to provide coverage or the equitable distribution of the loss, or the only identifiable personal protection insurance applicable to the injury is, because of financial inability of 1 or more insurers to fulfill their obligations, inadequate to provide benefits up to the maximum prescribed. In such case unpaid benefits due or coming due are subject to being collected under the assigned claims plan, and the insurer to which the claim is assigned, or the assigned

claims facility if the claim is assigned to it, is entitled to reimbursement from the defaulting insurers to the extent of their financial responsibility.

(2) Except as otherwise provided in this subsection, personal protection insurance benefits, including benefits arising from accidents occurring before the effective date of this subsection, payable through an assigned claims plan shall be reduced to the extent that benefits covering the same loss are available from other sources, regardless of the nature or number of benefit sources available and regardless of the nature or form of the benefits, to a person claiming personal protection insurance benefits through the assigned claims plan. This subsection shall only apply when the personal protection insurance benefits are payable through the assigned claims plan because no personal protection insurance is applicable to the injury, no personal protection insurance applicable to the injury can be identified, or the only identifiable personal protection insurance applicable to the injury is, because of financial inability of 1 or more insurers to fulfill their obligations, inadequate to provide benefits up to the maximum prescribed. As used in this subsection sources and benefit sources do not include the program for medical assistance for the medically indigent under the social welfare act, Act No. 280 of the Public Acts of 1939, being sections 400.1 to 400.121 of the Michigan Compiled Laws, or insurance under the health insurance for the aged act, title XVIII of the social security amendments of 1965.

(3) If the obligation to provide personal protection insurance benefits cannot be ascertained because of a dispute between 2 or more automobile insurers concerning their obligation to provide coverage or the equitable distribution of the loss, and if a method of voluntary payment of benefits cannot be agreed upon among or between the disputing insurers, all of the following shall apply:

(a) The insurers who are parties to the dispute shall, or the claimant may, immediately notify the assigned claims facility of their inability to determine their statutory obligations.

(b) The claim shall be assigned by the assigned claims facility to an insurer which shall immediately provide personal protection insurance benefits to the claimant or claimants entitled to benefits.

(c) An action shall be immediately commenced on behalf of the assigned claims facility by the insurer to whom the claim is assigned in circuit court for the purpose of declaring the rights and duties of any interested party.

(d) The insurer to whom the claim is assigned shall join as parties defendant each insurer disputing either the obligation to provide personal protection insurance benefits or the equitable distribution of the loss among the insurers.

(e) The circuit court shall declare the rights and duties of any interested party whether or not other relief is sought or could be granted.

(f) After hearing the action, the circuit court shall determine the insurer or insurers, if any, obligated to provide the applicable personal protection insurance benefits and the equitable distribution, if any, among the insurers obligated therefore, and shall order reimbursement to the assigned claims facility from the insurer or insurers to the extent of the responsibility as determined by the court. The reimbursement ordered under this subdivision shall include all benefits and costs paid or incurred by the assigned claims facility and all benefits and costs paid or incurred by insurers determined not to be obligated to provide applicable personal protection insurance benefits, including reasonable attorney fees and interest at the rate prescribed in section 3175 as of December 31 of the year preceding the determination of the circuit court.

**History:** Add. 1972, Act 294, Eff. Mar. 30, 1973 ;-- Am. 1972, Act 345, Imd. Eff. Jan. 9, 1973 ;-- Am. 1984, Act 426, Eff. Mar. 29, 1985

**Compiler's Notes:** Act 143 of 1993, which amended this section, was submitted to the people by referendum petition (as Proposal C) and rejected by a majority of the votes cast at the November 8, 1994, general election.

**Popular Name:** Act 218

**Popular Name:** Essential Insurance

**Popular Name:** No-Fault Insurance

## THE INSURANCE CODE OF 1956 (EXCERPT)

### Act 218 of 1956

## 500.3173 Certain persons disqualified from receiving benefits under assigned claims plans.

Sec. 3173.

A person who because of a limitation or exclusion in sections 3105 to 3116 is disqualified from receiving personal protection insurance benefits under a policy otherwise applying to his accidental bodily injury is also disqualified from receiving benefits under the assigned claims plan.

**History:** Add. 1972, Act 294, Eff. Mar. 30, 1973

**Popular Name:** Act 218

**Popular Name:** Essential Insurance

**Popular Name:** No-Fault Insurance

Â© 2004 Legislative Council, State of Michigan

# THE INSURANCE CODE OF 1956 (EXCERPT)

## Act 218 of 1956

**500.3173a    Eligibility    for    benefits;    initial determination; denial; notice.**

Sec. 3173a.

The assigned claims facility shall make an initial determination of the claimant's eligibility for benefits under the assigned claims plan and shall deny an obviously ineligible claim. The claimant shall be notified promptly in writing of the denial and the reasons for the denial.

**History:** Add. 1984, Act 426, Eff. Mar. 29, 1985

**Popular Name:** Act 218

**Popular Name:** Essential Insurance

**Popular Name:** No-Fault Insurance

# THE INSURANCE CODE OF 1956 (EXCERPT)

## Act 218 of 1956

**500.3174 Notice of claim through assigned claims plan; assignment of claim; notice to claimant; commencement of action by claimant.**

Sec. 3174.

A person claiming through an assigned claims plan shall notify the facility of his claim within the time that would have been allowed for filing an action for personal protection insurance benefits if identifiable coverage applicable to the claim had been in effect. The facility shall promptly assign the claim in accordance with the plan and notify the claimant of the identity and address of the insurer to which the claim is assigned, or of the facility if the claim is assigned to it. An action by the claimant shall not be commenced more than 30 days after receipt of notice of the assignment or the last date on which the action could have been commenced against an insurer of identifiable coverage applicable to the claim, whichever is later.

**History:** Add. 1972, Act 294, Eff. Mar. 30, 1973 ;-- Am. 1972, Act 345, Imd. Eff. Jan. 9, 1973

**Popular Name:** Act 218

**Popular Name:** Essential Insurance

**Popular Name:** No-Fault Insurance

© 2004 Legislative Council, State of Michigan

# THE INSURANCE CODE OF 1956 (EXCERPT)
## Act 218 of 1956

**500.3175 Rules for assignment of claims; duties of insurer to whom claims assigned; compromises and settlements; rules; limitation on action to enforce rights; interest on delinquent payments; installment payments.**

Sec. 3175.

(1) The assignment of claims shall be made according to rules that assure fair allocation of the burden of assigned claims among insurers doing business in this state on a basis reasonably related to the volume of automobile liability and personal protection insurance they write on motor vehicles or of the number of self-insured motor vehicles. An insurer to whom claims have been assigned shall make prompt payment of loss in accordance with this act and is thereupon entitled to reimbursement by the assigned claims facility for the payments and the established loss adjustment cost, together with an amount determined by use of the average annual 90-day United States treasury bill yield rate, as reported by the council of economic advisers as of December 31 of the year for which reimbursement is sought, as follows:

(a) For the calendar year in which claims are paid by the insurer, the amount shall be determined by applying the specified annual yield rate specified in this subsection to 1/2 of the total claims payments and loss adjustment costs.

(b) For the period from the end of the calendar year in which claims are paid by the insurer to the date payments for the operation of the assigned claims facility and the assigned claims plan are due, the amount will be determined by applying the annual yield rate specified in this subsection to the total claims payments and loss adjustment costs multiplied by a fraction the denominator of which is 365 and the numerator of which is equal to the number of days that have elapsed between the end of the calendar year and the date payments for the operation of the assigned claims facility and the assigned claims plan are due.

(2) The insurer to whom claims have been assigned shall preserve and enforce rights to indemnity or reimbursement against third parties and account to the assigned claims facility therefor and shall assign such rights to the assigned claims facility upon reimbursement by the assigned claims facility. This section shall not preclude an insurer from entering into reasonable compromises and settlements with third parties against whom rights to indemnity or reimbursement exist. The insurer shall account to the assigned claims facility for such compromises and settlements. The rules promulgated under section 3171 shall include a rule establishing reasonable standards for enforcing rights to indemnity or reimbursement against third parties, including a standard establishing a value for such rights below which actions to preserve and enforce the rights need not be pursued.

(3) An action to enforce rights to indemnity or reimbursement against a third party shall not be commenced after the later of 2 years after the assignment of the claim to the insurer or 1 year after the date of the last payment to the claimant.

(4) Payments for the operation of the assigned claims facility and plan not paid by the due date shall bear interest at the rate of 20% per annum.

(5) The secretary of state through the facility may enter into a written agreement with the debtor permitting the payment of the judgment or acknowledgment of debt in installments payable to the facility.

**History:** Add. 1972, Act 294, Eff. Mar. 30, 1973 ;-- Am. 1972, Act 345, Imd. Eff. Jan. 9, 1973 ;-- Am. 1984, Act 426, Eff. Mar. 29, 1985

**Popular Name:** Act 218

**Popular Name:** Essential Insurance

**Popular Name:** No-Fault Insurance

# THE INSURANCE CODE OF 1956 (EXCERPT)

## Act 218 of 1956

## 500.3176 Taking costs into account in making and regulating rates.

Sec. 3176.

Reasonable costs incurred in the handling and disposition of assigned claims, including amounts paid pursuant to assessments under section 3171, shall be taken into account in making and regulating rates for automobile liability and personal protection insurance.

**History:** Add. 1972, Act 294, Eff. Mar. 30, 1973 ;-- Am. 1972, Act 345, Imd. Eff. Jan. 9, 1973

**Popular Name:** Act 218

**Popular Name:** Essential Insurance

**Popular Name:** No-Fault Insurance

Â© 2004 Legislative Council, State of Michigan

# THE INSURANCE CODE OF 1956 (EXCERPT)

## Act 218 of 1956

### 500.3177 Recovery by insurer of benefits and costs from owner or registrant of uninsured motor vehicle; written agreement to pay judgment in installments; notice.

Sec. 3177.

(1) An insurer obligated to pay personal protection insurance benefits for accidental bodily injury to a person arising out of the ownership, maintenance, or use of an uninsured motor vehicle as a motor vehicle may recover such benefits paid and appropriate loss adjustment costs incurred from the owner or registrant of the uninsured motor vehicle or from his or her estate. Failure of such a person to make payment within 30 days after judgment is a ground for suspension or revocation of his or her motor vehicle registration and license as defined in section 25 of the Michigan vehicle code, Act No. 300 of the Public Acts of 1949, being section 257.25 of the Michigan Compiled Laws. An uninsured motor vehicle for the purpose of this section is a motor vehicle with respect to which security is required by sections 3101 and 3102 is not in effect at the time of the accident.

(2) The motor vehicle registration and license shall not be suspended or revoked and the motor vehicle registration and license shall be restored if the debtor enters into a written agreement with the secretary

of state permitting the payment of the judgment in installments, if the payment of any installments is not in default.

(3) The secretary of state upon receipt of a certified abstract of court record of a judgment or notice from the insurer of an acknowledgment of debt shall notify the owner or registrant of an uninsured vehicle of the provisions of subsection (1) at that person's last recorded address with the secretary of state and inform that person of the right to enter into a written agreement with the secretary of state for the payment of the judgment or debt in installments.

**History:** Add. 1972, Act 294, Eff. Mar. 30, 1973 ;-- Am. 1984, Act 426, Eff. Mar. 29, 1985

**Popular Name:** Act 218

**Popular Name:** Essential Insurance

**Popular Name:** No-Fault Insurance

Â© 2004 Legislative Council, State of Michigan

# THE INSURANCE CODE OF 1956 (EXCERPT)
# Act 218 of 1956

## 500.3179 Act applicable October 1, 1973.

Sec. 3179.

This act applies to motor vehicle accidents occurring on or after October 1, 1973.

**History:** Add. 1972, Act 294, Eff. Mar. 30, 1973

**Popular Name:** Act 218

**Popular Name:** Essential Insurance

**Popular Name:** No-Fault Insurance

---

*The Educated Consumers Guide to No-Fault Automobile Insurance*

STATE OF MICHIGAN JENNIFER M. GRANHOLM GOVERNOR
**OFFICE OF FINANCIAL AND INSURANCE SERVICES** DEPARTMENT OF LABOR & ECONOMIC GROWTH DAVID C. HOLLISTER, DIRECTOR LINDA A. WATTERS COMMISSIONER

# *Michigan Catastrophic Claims Association (MCCA)*

## Updated March 17, 2005

### What is the Michigan Catastrophic Claims Association (MCCA)?

Michigan is the only state that offers unlimited personal injury protection benefits. These benefits are offered through no-fault auto insurance policies. The Michigan Catastrophic Claims Association (MCCA) reimburses no-fault auto insurers for benefits that exceed $375,000, as of July 1, 2005. MCCA was created by the legislature as a means of spreading costs across all Michigan motorists for providing these unique unlimited benefits.

Although created by statute, the MCCA is a private, nonprofit association. All of its dealings are with insurance companies, not the general public. The MCCA has a Board of Directors that consists of 5 representatives from insurance companies, appointed by the Commissioner of the Office of Financial and Insurance Services (OFIS) according to statute. The insurance companies appointed to serve on this board are among the top writers, by volume of business, of

161

auto insurance in Michigan. The Commissioner of OFIS serves as an ex-officio member of the board without a vote.

# How is the MCCA assessment determined?

Each year, the MCCA analyzes the amount needed to cover the lifetime claims of all people catastrophically injured in a car accident. This analysis includes review of the investment return that the fund receives, medical cost inflation, and any changes to coverages. The analysis yields an amount needed to pay those lifetime claims and a per vehicle assessment is set based on that amount.

Since July 1, 1978, when the fund was started, 18,000 catastrophic claims have been reported to the MCCA. Based on current estimates, more than 10,220 claims remain active, resulting in future lifetime payments in excess of $47 billion. This figure assumes inflating costs for products, services, and accommodations necessary for the care, recovery and rehabilitation of injured persons throughout their lives. The MCCA further estimates that an additional 1,500 Michigan insured will be catastrophically injured in auto accidents next year. It is the cost of providing these medical benefits that influences the MCCA assessment.

How is the MCCA funded?

An MCCA assessment is charged to every Michigan auto insurance premium. The assessment funds a pool of money for medical costs exceeding

$375,000, as of July 1, 2005, resulting from an auto accident.

Do I pay this assessment?

Although the MCCA assessment technically is made to the insurance company, companies typically pass the assessment on to policyholders. Some insurance companies include the MCCA assessment in the Personal Injury Protection (PIP) portion of your insurance premium. Other companies sometimes list this as a "statutory assessment" or "MCCA assessment" on the declarations page of your policy.

Even though the amount assessed each insurer by the MCCA is the same, each company may include administrative and other miscellaneous costs in the amount it assesses policyholders for this coverage. Therefore, the amount assessed by the MCCA may affect each policyholder's premium differently. If you have questions about the amount being assessed, you may wish to contact your insurance agent or insurance company.

What is the assessment for 2005?

The MCCA announced that the 2005 assessment will be $141.70. The pure premium (the actual cost for each vehicle in the state of Michigan to fund the MCCA pool) is $116.43 and the deficit adjustment is $25.17, with a $.10 administrative expense, setting the assessment at $141.70.

What will happen to the assessment in the future?

The MCCA Board meets every spring to set the assessment for the year beginning

July 1st. The assessment is set using the same criteria – by analyzing the amount needed to cover the lifetime claims of all people catastrophically injured in a car accident. Investment return, medical cost inflation, and any changes to coverage will again be considered.

Do I pay the full assessment if I own a historic vehicle?

Public Act 662 of 2002 reduced the MCCA assessment for historic vehicles to 20 percent of the full assessment charged for vehicles effective July 1, 2003. The assessment for historic vehicles beginning July 1, 2005 will be $28.34.

More information on Michigan auto insurance:

OFIS always recommends that Michigan citizens shop around for their auto insurance –a range of prices is available depending on many factors like discounts offered by insurance companies or coverage levels. The "2004" Buyer's Guide to Auto Insurance in Michigan" assists in the shopping process by providing estimates from insurance companies. The guide is available from the OFIS web site at: http://www.cis.state.mi.us/fis/ pubs/guides/auto/auto_buyer_criteria.asp

In addition, the "Consumer's Guide to No-Fault Automobile Insurance in Michigan" brochure provides more information on auto insurance. You can obtain this brochure from the OFIS web site at:

www.michigan.gov/documents/cis_ofis_autogd_no_
fault_24054_7.pdf . The above mentioned guide and
brochure are also available by calling OFIS toll free at

877-999-6442. Consumer assistance is also available
at this toll free number if you have questions about the
MCCA or need assistance on any matters of insurance,
banking, lending and securities.


Michigan Catastrophic Claims Association (MCCA)

Information as of March 17, 2005

Since July 1, 1978 when the fund was started, 18,000
claims have been reported to the MCCA. A claim
represents the auto accident that caused the catastrophic
injury - it does not represent the number of people
injured. Most claims, but not all, include only one
person.

## MICHIGAN CATASTROPHIC CLAIMS ASSOCIATION ASSESSMENT HISTORY

| Assmt # | Pure Period | (Surplus) Months | | Admin. Deficit Adj. | Total Assessment |
|---|---|---|---|---|---|
| 1 | 7/1/78 to 6/30/79 | 12 | $3.00 | $0.00 | $3.00 |
| 2 | 7/1/79 to 12/31/79 | 6 | $6.28 | $5.40 | $11.68 |
| 3 | 1/1/80 to 12/31/80 | 12 | $6.36 | ($0.36) | $6.00 |
| 4 | 1/1/81 to 12/31/81 | 12 | $7.14 | ($0.58) | $6.76 |
| 5 | 1/1/82 to 12/31/82 | 12 | $6.64 | ($0.81) | $5.93 |
| 6 | 1/1/83 to 12/31/83 | 12 | $7.55 | ($2.12) | $5.53 |
| 7 | 1/1/84 to 12/31/84 | 12 | $8.24 | ($2.44) | $5.91 |
| 8 | 1/1/85 to 12/31/85 | 12 | $10.55 | $1.40 | $12.05 |
| 9 | 1/1/86 to 12/31/86 | 12 | $11.24 | $3.07 | $14.40 |

| | Period | | | | | |
|---|---|---|---|---|---|---|
| 10 | 1/1/87 to 12/31/87 | 12 | $15.77 | $6.81 | $0.09 | $22.67 |
| 11 | 1/1/88 to 12/31/88 | 12 | $24.41 | $8.10 | $0.09 | $32.60 |
| 12 | 1/1/89 to 12/31/89 | 12 | $33.44 | $10.12 | $0.09 | $43.65 |
| 13 | 1/1/90 to 12/31/90 | 12 | $48.12 | $18.37 | $0.15 | $66.64 |
| 14 | 1/1/91 to 12/31/91 | 12 | $68.33 | $32.50 | $0.17 | $101.00 |
| 15 | 1/1/92 to 12/31/92 | 12 | $77.69 | $32.77 | $0.12 | $110.58 |
| 16 | 1/1/93 to 12/31/93 | 12 | $90.43 | $28.14 | $0.12 | $118.69 |
| 17 | 1/1/94 to 12/31/94 | 12 | $98.71 | $16.89 | $0.12 | $115.72 |
| 18 | 1/1/95 to 12/31/95 | 12 | $98.07 | ($1.24) | $0.12 | $96.95 |
| 19 | 1/1/96 to 12/31/96 | 12 | $87.53 | ($15.06) | $0.10 | $72.57 |
| 20 | 1/1/97 to 12/31/97 | 12 | $62.03 | ($47.19) | $0.10 | $14.94 |

| | | | | | | |
|---|---|---|---|---|---|---|
| 21 | 1/1/98 to 12/31/98 | 12 | $63.87 | ($58.37) | $0.10 | $5.60 |
| 22 | 1/1/99 to 12/31/99 | 12 | $56.31 | ($50.81) | $0.10 | $5.60 |
| 23 | 1/1/00 to 12/31/00 | 12 | $52.30 | ($46.79) | $0.09 | $5.60 |
| 24 | 1/1/01 to 12/31/01 | 12 | $61.53 | ($47.21) | $0.09 | $14.41 |
| 25 | 1/1/02 to 06/30/02 | 6 | $71.05 | $0.00 | $0.10 | $71.15 |
| 26 | 7/1/02 to 6/30/03 | 12 | $68.90 | $0.00 | $0.10 | $69.00 |
| 27 | 7/1/03 to 6/30/04 | 12 | $79.30 | $20.80 | $0.10 | $100.20 |
| 28 | 7/1/04 to 6/30/05 | 12 | $95.93 | $31.21 | $0.10 | $127.24 |
| 29 | 7/1/05 to 6/30/06 | 12 | $116.43 | $25.17 | $0.10 | $141.70 |

JOHN G. PROSSER II
Vice President
Development, Acquisition
& Public Relations

3345 Auburn Rd
Suite 206
Rochester Hills, MI 48309
1 (888) 299-9800
FAX (248) 299-9804

Grand Rapids (800) 590-7886
Southfield (800) 969-7723
Flint (800) 644-1250

HI-TECH INC.

# Michigan Jaycees Prepare For New Leadership and Training

## Brain Injury Prevention

Pediatric brain injury and the accompanying trauma is the leading cause of death and disability to children in America today. Ninety percent could be prevented by the use of safety helmets!

Starting in May 1995, the Michigan Jaycees launched an educational campaign throughout the state, encouraging members to share information regarding the danger and consequences of not wearing a safety helmet.

*I need your help.* As a local chapter member and leader you can make a massive contribution toward the safety and health of our children by getting involved in this campaign.

In November of 1995, thirty thousand fact sheet flyers were distributed in every student in the Pontiac school system. The flyer invited students and families to a magic show. The magic show was used as a fund-raiser for the Brain Injury Association (BIA) "Billboard Campaign." It featured Scorpio and Fantasy (810-749-5451) who have agreed to do fund-raiser for 50 percent of revenue! If you do this fund-raiser, and were to gross $5,000, half is $2,000 goes to the BIA!

*Here is what I need!*

• Distribute "bright orange fact sheets." Please call me or fax me your address and the number of flyers you would like.

• You can get a radio interview (copy to broadcast as a public service announcement) 1/2 hour show outlines the facts and strategies of the Michigan Jaycees.

• You can generate local press releases, conduct fund-raisers, recruit local citizens to join Jaycees and become block captains and distribute fact sheets door-to-door!!

For 1997, we are working on several things. One plan is to "piggy-back" our campaign with the Chrysler Corporation's campaign to educate children nationwide to wear seatbelts. We also hope to get money from the Lions for the billboard campaign. Gannett Outdoors has donated 3,000 spots (we must pay for the paper). We are also working with McDonald's to get a designer paper tray liner for their restaurants. And we are working with Nike to produce a PSA on TV and have a commitment from Nickelodeon and MTV to air it. 1997 will hopefully see a celebrity dinner fund-raiser, as well as a TV special which highlights this issue. We hope to broadcast this documentary on a national basis, raising public awareness, money for research and prevention, and let's not forget the added bonus of recruiting new members to the Jaycees.

Lastly, I am available to speak at Region meetings and promise a passionate, informative and brief presentation. Please contact me with advance notice of at least 3 weeks. The important numbers are: work: 810-431-3465; work: 810-423-3466 or 800-969-7723; home fax: 810-335-0599; or write to me at 541 West Iroquois, Pontiac, MI 48341.

May God bless you and yours in 1997.

Very truly yours in Jaycees,
John G. Prosser, II
MIJC State Chairman, JCI Senator #48806, Past Chairman, Pontiac Jaycees, Vice President, Health Partners, Southfield

169

## *John Gwynne Prosser II*

I have spent 4 years as Co-Owner and Vice President of Government Entitlement Services.

GES was a company which provided win/win cost containment services to America's largest insurance companies by providing patient advocacy for insured's before the social security administration by pursuing claimant's social security disability benefits. GES maintained 6 offices across America, and it was during this experience that I became aware of the challenging needs of the catastrophically injured. A significant number of Automobile insurers in Michigan which were GES clients, indicated that one of their biggest challenge was finding competent services for insured's who required homecare nursing services 24 hours per day 7 days per week. It occurred to me that a new business model different than the Medicare model of visits was needed. I left GES and joined Health Partners.

I joined Health Partners as Vice President of development, acquisitions and public relations to build the model for specialized homecare nursing services for the brain and spinal cord injured. This population presented a large challenge and a significant opportunity, if their needs could be satisfied. I saw a huge opportunity and today Health Partners is the largest company of its kind in Michigan. Mr. Michael Gillet the President and Founder of Health Partners, and my business partner in other enterprises as well, shared my vision for creating an organization that supported and educated home health aides to deal with the complex issues involved in this care for automobile accident victims. All of our companies are dedicated to excellence in service. Mr. Richard Brown is also an Owner of Health Partners and the cornerstone of our companies. Mrs. Mary Slago our Vice President of Nursing deserves acknowledgement as well for her innovative Nursing leadership.

I am also a Partner in Health Providers Choice a National Nurse Staffing Agency which provides Registered Nurses to Hospitals on a contract basis. I am a Partner with Ms. Rose Torrento, Mr. Richard Brown, and Mr. Michael Gillet

I am also a Partner in The Grand Home of Marshall a residence for the Brain and Spinal Cord injured. I am a Partner with Mrs. Mary Slago, Mr. Richard Brown, and Mr. Michael Gillet.

I am also a Partner in HP Personnel, a Staffing agency serving many categories of need mostly outside of healthcare. I am a Partner with Mr. Michael Gillet and Mr. Richard Brown.

I wish to acknowledge my Partners as the creative and dynamic people that they are and thank all of them for sharing their expertise and enthusiasm with me and allowing me to share my expertise and enthusiasm with them. We are all engaged in the engrossing and satisfying work of serving the needs of people who have tremendous challenges. We are all dedicated to excellent service and compassionate care for people with significant medical conditions both in the Home and in Hospitals.

\*\*I wish to thank and acknowledge my Wife for her support, encouragement and typing skills! Tessie Prosser, I love you!

John Gwynne Prosser II

Has 18 years of Health Care Services experience including acute care, long term care, home health care, insurance cost containment, and facility staffing services, as well as an administrator of mobile ultrasound services.

Mr. Prosser has successfully expanded Health Partners Homecare services statewide in Michigan through his passion for excellence and his commitment to customer service as well as attention to details in a highly subjective and specialized service industry.

Mr. Prosser understands the auto no-fault insurance scheme for Michigan and has been a regular presenter to case management groups, social workers, insurance adjusters, attorney's and the Brain injury association and other groups in the Health care arena.

Mr. Prosser is a contributor to the Aetna case management guidelines project.

Mr. Prosser has served as the National Chairman for Pediatric Brain Injury Prevention, for the United States Junior Chamber of Commerce, Senate. As Chairman he was able to persuade President George Herbert Walker Bush to produce a public service announcement on video to help promote awareness and reduce injury, by encouraging the use of helmets for children and adults during sporting activities.

Mr. Prosser has been active in community service for 26 years and is a Junior Chamber International Senator and a founding member of the International Business Network of the JCI.

Mr. Prosser is a Past President of the Pontiac Jaycees

Mr. Prosser is a Past President of the Pontiac Chamber of Commerce, having been its founder as the President of the Pontiac Business Association.

You can contact John via email at-

 JPROSSER123@comcast.net  or JGP2@comcast.net

Or you can write to him at:

3345 Auburn Road #206,

Rochester Hills, MI 48309

Printed in the United States
83054LV00001B/1-99/A

9 781420 859485